THE OPTIONS PLAYBOOK™

TABLE OF CONTENTS:

WELCOME TO THE GAME

INTRODUCTION

BY BRIAN "THE OPTIONS GUY" OVERBY
TradeKing Senior Options Analyst

OPTION TRADING is a way for savvy investors to leverage assets and control some of the risks associated with playing the market. Pretty much every investor is familiar with the saying, "Buy low and sell high." But with options, it's possible to profit whether stocks are going up, down, or sideways. You can use options to cut losses, protect gains, and control large chunks of stock with a relatively small cash outlay.

On the other hand, options can be complicated and risky. Not only might you lose your entire investment, some strategies may expose you to theoretically unlimited losses.

So before you trade options, it's important to think about the effects that variables like implied volatility and time decay will have on your strategy. This playbook will help you answer those tough questions. No need to ponder, just turn to the play.

I'm not going to derive the Black-Scholes option pricing model in this book. As a matter of fact, this is one of the only times I even mention the Black-Scholes model. It's nice to know that sort of thing, but the goal here is to provide the essential knowledge needed to trade a specific strategy, not to completely bore the pants off of you.

Throughout this playbook, you'll also find "Options Guy's Tips," which clarify essential concepts or give you extra advice on how to run a particular play. As an indicator of these tips' importance, I put a little picture of my head next to them like the one you see at left. So be sure to pay extra attention whenever you see my melon.

I certainly hope you enjoy reading *The Options Playbook*.

Brian Overby

JUMP IN, THE WATER'S FINE

For rookies, I've created a brief overview of how options work, and outlined some plays to help you get started. These strategies will help familiarize you with the option market without leaving your proverbial backside overexposed to risk.

Don't get me wrong, however. All option trades involve risk and are not suited to all investors. Option contracts usually represent 100 shares of stock, so be careful. You should avoid trading more options than the number of shares you're used to.

If you typically trade 100 shares of stock, trade one option contract. If you typically trade 200 shares, trade two option contracts, and so on. (Get used to hearing me say that last bit. I'll be repeating it often, and for good reason.)

STAY MENTALLY TOUGH OUT THERE

For more experienced option traders, I hope this playbook will serve as a convenient reference tool. Here, you'll find the construction and risk profiles for many different strategies. That means you can stay focused on forecasting or analyzing "The Greeks," instead of experiencing brain strain while trying to remember exactly how to calculate your break-even points or set up an iron condor.

For each play, I've pointed out key indicators to look for using the option tools on TradeKing.com. These tools can be an invaluable resource for option traders. So remember to use them as much as possible. (Tattooing our URL on the back of your hand might help in this regard.)

I'll be honest, you're not going to reap wind-fall profits every time. So don't dig fingernail marks into your desk or tear out clumps of your hair every time you're about to get hit with a loss. Sometimes you make money and sometimes you lose money. It's all part of the game. The idea is simply to run the right plays, and win more often than you lose.

LET'S GET BUSY

I'm not going to overload you with minute details about how the option market works, how options are priced and that kind of thing. There are already plenty of textbooks out there designed to do that. So we'll just touch briefly on those topics and then stay focused on the knowledge you need to run the 40 option plays in this book.

If you're still hungry for knowledge when you get to the end, head to TradeKing.com and visit our learning center. There's plenty there to satisfy even the most gargantuan mind.

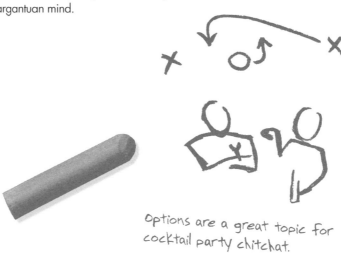

Options are a great topic for cocktail party chitchat.

GOOD PLACES TO STUDY THIS PLAYBOOK

- IN AN AIRPLANE
- IN A CAR (AS LONG AS YOU'RE NOT DRIVING)
- BY THE POOL
- ON THE CAN
- IN BED
- IN A WAITING ROOM
- AT WORK
- ON THE TRAIN
- AT YOUR COMPUTER WHILE TRADING ON TRADEKING.COM
- WHILE SIPPING A COCKTAIL

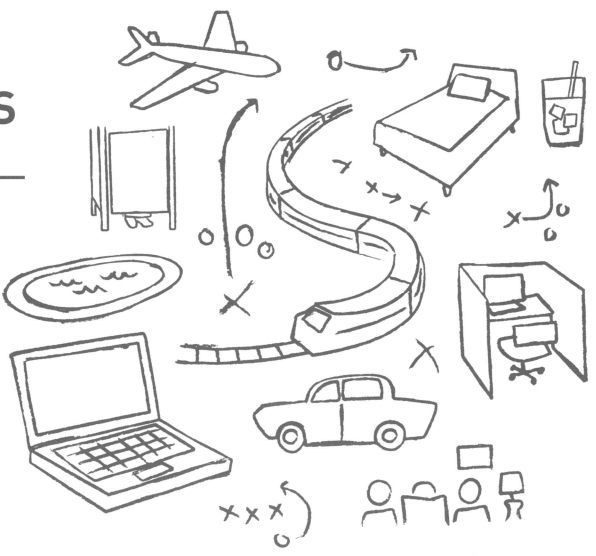

BAD PLACE TO STUDY THIS PLAYBOOK

- **ON A TRAMPOLINE**

THE LONG AND SHORT OF THINGS

TAKING STOCK OF THE SITUATION

HERE are a few things you absolutely need to understand before this playbook will make as much sense to you as I hope it will. Some of you probably already know these terms and concepts, or at least think you do. But how will you really know you know them unless you read this section? Therein lies the paradox.

Of course, if you're a seasoned veteran or MVP, by all means skip right ahead to the plays. And for you Rookies, well, read on. I'll try to keep it interesting.

THROUGHOUT THIS BOOK I talk about the "stock" that options are based on. That's a bit of an oversimplification. Actually, options can be traded on several kinds of underlying securities. Some of the most common ones are stocks, indexes, or ETFs (Exchange Traded Funds). So feel free to substitute these terms to match your preferred style of trading.

WHAT'S AN OPTION?

OPTIONS ARE CONTRACTS giving the owner the right to buy or sell an asset at a fixed price (called the "strike price") for a specific period of time. That period of time could be as short as a day or as long as a couple of years, depending on the option. The seller of the option contract has the obligation to take the opposite side of the trade if and when the owner exercises the right to buy or sell the asset.

Here's an example of a standard quote on an option.

Contracts
    gives right to buy or sell

XYZ   an asset at

$70   a strike price

JANUARY for a specified amt of time

$3.10   FOR A GIVEN AMT OF money

That's the stock that the option is based on. Not an indication your fly is down. It usually represents 100 shares.

That's the "strike price" for the stock. So the stock will change hands at $70 if the option is exercised.

That's the "premium," or per-share cost of the option. Option contracts usually represent 100 shares of the underlying stock, so you'll actually pay $310 plus commission for this contract. ($3.10 x 100 = $310)

XYZ JANUARY 70 CALL AT $3.10

That's the month the option expires. The last day to trade the option is usually the third Friday of this month.

That's the type of option. There are two kinds of options: calls and puts. They're defined on the next pages.

THE TWO FLAVORS OF OPTIONS: CALLS & PUTS

CALL OPTIONS

When you *buy* a call, it gives you the right (but not the obligation) to buy a specific stock at a specific price per share within a specific time frame. A good way to remember this is: you have the right to "call" the stock away from somebody.

If you *sell* a call, you have the obligation to sell the stock at a specific price per share within a specific time frame if the call buyer decides to invoke the right to buy the stock at that price.

BUY a CALL
right to BUY

SELL A CALL
obligation to SELL

Call options
give you the right to
call stock away from someone

PUT OPTIONS

When you *buy* a put, it gives you the right (but not the obligation) to sell a specific stock at a specific price per share within a specific time frame. A good way to remember this is: you have the right to "put" stock to somebody.

If you *sell* a put, you have the obligation to buy the stock at a specific price per share within a specific time frame if the put buyer decides to invoke the right to sell the stock at that price.

BUY a PUT
right to sell

SELL A PUT
obligation to BUY

Put options
give you the right to
put stock to someone

Much of the time, individual calls and puts are not used as a standalone strategy. They can be combined with stock positions, and/or other calls and puts based on the same stock.

When this is the case, the strategies are called "complex." This term does not imply they are hard to understand. It just means these plays are built from multiple options, and may at times also include a stock position.

You'll find out about the various uses of calls and puts when we examine specific plays later in the book.

DEFINITELY-NOT-BORING
DEFINITIONS

Don't worry if some of these meanings aren't crystal clear at first. That's normal. Just keep forging ahead, and everything will become more apparent over time.

LONG – This term can be pretty confusing. In this book, it usually doesn't refer to time. As in, "TradeKing never leaves me on hold for long." Or distance, as in, "I went for a long jog."

When you're talking about options and stocks, "long" implies a position of ownership. After you have purchased an option or a stock, you are considered to be long that security in your account.

SHORT – Short is another one of those words you have to be careful about. It doesn't refer to your hair after a buzz cut, or that time at camp when you short-sheeted your counselor's bed.

If you've sold an option or a stock without actually owning it, you are then considered to be "short" that security in your account. That's one of the interesting things about options. You can sell something that you don't actually own. But when you do, you may be obligated to do something at a later date. As you read through this book, you'll get a clearer picture of what that something might be for specific plays.

STRIKE PRICE – The pre-agreed price per share at which stock may be bought or sold under the terms of an option contract. I've mentioned strike price a couple of times already, but I just want to make sure I hammer the definition home. Some people refer to the strike price as the "exercise price."

IN-THE-MONEY (ITM) – For call options, this means the stock price is above the strike price. So if a call has a strike price of $50 and the stock is trading at $55, that option is in-the-money.

For put options, it means the stock price is below the strike price. So if a put has a strike price of $50 and the stock is trading at $45, that option is in-the-money.

This term might also remind you of a great song from the 1930s that you can tap dance to whenever your option plays go according to plan.

OUT-OF-THE-MONEY (OTM) – For call options, this means the stock price is below the strike price. For put options, this means the stock price is above the strike price. The cost of out-of-the-money options consists entirely of "time value."

AT-THE-MONEY (ATM) – An option is "at-the-money" when the stock price is equal to the strike price. (Since the two values are rarely exactly equal, when purchasing options the strike price closest to the stock price is typically called the "ATM strike.")

INTRINSIC VALUE – The amount an option is in-the-money. Obviously, only in-the-money options have intrinsic value.

TIME VALUE – The part of an option price that is based on its time to expiration. If you subtract the amount of intrinsic value from an option price, you're left with the time value. If an option has no intrinsic value (i.e., it's out-of-the-money) its entire worth is based on time value.

I would also like to take this opportunity to say while you're reading this book you're spending your time valuably.

EXERCISE – This occurs when the owner of an option invokes the right embedded in the option contract. In layman's terms, it means the option owner buys or sells the underlying stock at the strike price, and requires the option seller to take the other side of the trade.

Interestingly, options are a lot like most people, in that exercise is a fairly infrequent event. (See "Cashing Out Your Options," on P.23.)

ASSIGNMENT – When an option owner exercises the option, an option seller (or "writer") is assigned and must make good on his or her obligation. That means he or she is required to buy or sell the underlying stock at the strike price.

INDEX OPTIONS VS. EQUITY OPTIONS – In this book, I occasionally make reference to index options. There are a few differences between index options and equity options, and it's important for you to understand them. First, index options typically can't be exercised prior to expiration, whereas equity options typically can. Second, the last day to trade most index options is the Thursday before the third Friday of the expiration month. (That's not always the third Thursday of the month. It might actually be the second Thursday if the month started on a Friday.) But the last day to trade equity options is the third Friday of the expiration month. Third, index options are cash-settled, but equity options result in stock changing hands.

NOTE: There are several exceptions to these general guidelines about index options. If you're going to trade an index, you must take the time to understand its characteristics. See "So What's an Index Option Anyhow?" on P.145. And to find out more, visit cboe.com or ask a TradeKing broker.

STOP-LOSS ORDER - An order to sell a stock or option when it reaches a certain price (the stop price). The order is designed to help limit an investor's exposure to the markets on an existing position.

Here's how a stop-loss order works: first you select a stop price, usually below the current market price for an existing long position. By choosing a price below the current market, you're basically saying, "This is the downside point where I would like to get out of my position."

Past this price, you no longer want the cheese; you just want out of the trap. When your position trades at or through your stop price, your stop order will get activated as a market order, seeking the best available market price at that time the order is triggered to close out your position.

A word to the wise...any discussion of stop orders isn't complete without mentioning this caveat: they do not provide much protection if the market is closed or trading is halted during the day. In those situations, stocks are likely to gap – that is, the next trade price after the trading halt might be significantly different from the prices before the halt. If the stock gaps, your downside "protective" order will most likely trigger, but it's anybody's guess as to what the next available price will be.

STANDARD DEVIATION – This is a book about options, not statistics. But I'll be using this term a lot, so I should clarify its meaning a little. Here's the short and sweet version.

If we assume stocks have a simple normal price distribution, we can calculate what a one standard deviation move for the stock will be. On an annualized basis the stock will stay within plus or minus one standard deviation roughly 68% of the time. This comes in handy when figuring out the potential range of movement for a particular stock. I'll tell you more later about how to determine just how many dollars a one standard deviation move would be for a particular stock.

NOTE: For simplicity's sake, here I assume a normal distribution. Most pricing models assume a log normal distribution. Just in case you're a Statistician or something.

WHAT IS VOLATILITY?

OR WHY YOUR OPTION PRICES CAN BE LESS STABLE THAN A ONE-LEGGED DUCK

Some traders mistakenly believe that volatility is based on a directional trend in the stock price. Not so. By definition, volatility is simply the amount the stock price fluctuates, without regard for direction.

As an individual trader, you really only need to concern yourself with two forms of volatility: historical volatility and implied volatility. (Unless your temper gets particularly volatile when a trade goes against you, in which case you should probably worry about that, too.)

HISTORICAL VOLATILITY is defined in textbooks as "the annualized standard deviation of past stock price movements." But since this isn't your average textbook and I don't want to bore you silly, I'll just say it's how much the stock price fluctuated on a day-to-day basis over a one-year period.

Even if a $100 stock winds up at exactly $100 one year from now, it still could have a great deal of historical volatility. After all, it's certainly conceivable that the stock could have traded as high as $175 or as low as $25 at some point. And if there were wide daily price ranges throughout the year, it would indeed be considered a historically volatile stock.

FIGURE 1: **HISTORICAL VOLATILITY OF TWO DIFFERENT STOCKS**

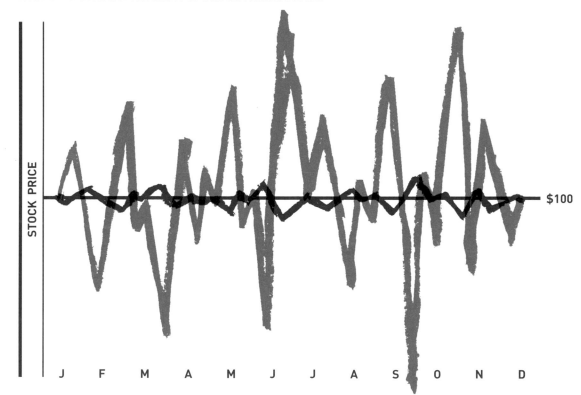

This chart shows the historical pricing of two different stocks over 12 months. They both start at $100 and end at $100. However, the blue line shows a great deal of historical volatility while the black line does not.

IMPLIED VOLATILITY isn't based on historical pricing data on the stock. Instead, it's what the marketplace is "implying" the volatility of the stock will be in the future, based on the price of an option. Like historical volatility, this figure is expressed on an annualized basis. But implied volatility is typically of more interest to retail option traders than historical volatility because it is forward-looking rather than concerned with the past.

WHERE DOES IMPLIED VOLATILITY COME FROM? (HINT: NOT THE STORK)

Based on truth and rumors in the marketplace, option prices will begin to change. If there's an earnings announcement or a major court decision coming up, traders will alter trading patterns on certain options. That drives the price of those options up or down, independent of stock price movement. Keep in mind, it's not the options' intrinsic value (if any) that is changing. Only the options' time value is affected.

The reason the options' time value will change is because of changes in the perceived potential range of future price movement on the stock. Implied volatility can then be derived from the cost of the option. In fact, if there were no options traded on a given stock, there would be no way to calculate implied volatility.

IMPLIED VOLATILITY AND OPTION PRICES

Implied volatility is a dynamic figure that changes based on activity in the options marketplace. Usually, when implied volatility increases, the price of options will increase as well, assuming all other things remain constant. So when implied volatility increases after a trade has been placed, it's good for the option owner and bad for the option seller.

Conversely, if implied volatility decreases after your trade is placed, the price of options usually decreases. That's good if you're an option seller and bad if you're an option owner.

In the next section of this playbook, titled "Meet the Greeks," I'm going to introduce you to a factor called "vega" that can help you calculate how much option prices are expected to change when implied volatility changes. But for now, let's stay focused on how implied volatility relates to potential movement of the stock price.

HOW IMPLIED VOLATILITY CAN HELP YOU ESTIMATE POTENTIAL RANGE OF MOVEMENT ON A STOCK

Implied volatility is expressed as a percentage of the stock price, indicating a one standard deviation move over the course of a year. For those of you who snoozed through Statistics 101, a stock should end up within one standard deviation of its original price 68% of the time during the upcoming 12 months. It will end up within two standard deviations 95% of the time and within three standard deviations 99% of the time.

FIGURE 2: **NORMAL DISTRIBUTION OF STOCK PRICE**

Stock = **$50**
Implied Volatility = **20%**

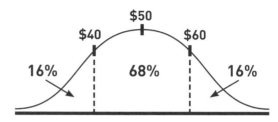

In theory, there's a 68% probability that a stock trading at $50 with an implied volatility of 20% will cost between $40 and $60 a year later. There's also a 16% chance it will be above $60 and a 16% chance it will be below $40. But remember, the operative words are "in theory," since implied volatility isn't an exact science.

For simplicity's sake, I'm going to focus on the one standard deviation move, which you can think of as a dividing line between "probable" and "not-so-probable."

For example, imagine stock XYZ is trading at $50, and the implied volatility of an option contract is 20%. This implies there's a consensus in the marketplace that a one standard deviation move over the next 12 months will be plus or minus $10 (since 20% of the $50 stock price equals $10).

So here's what it all boils down to: the marketplace thinks there's a 68% chance at the end of one year that XYZ will wind up somewhere between $40 and $60.

By extension, that also means there's only a 32% chance the stock will be outside this range. 16% of the time it should be above $60, and 16% of the time it should be below $40. (See figure 2, where this is all laid out neatly for you.)

Obviously, knowing the probability of the underlying stock finishing within a certain range at expiration is very important when determining what options you want to buy or sell and when figuring out which strategies you might want to implement.

Just remember: implied volatility is based on general consensus in the marketplace – it's not an infallible predictor of stock movement. After all, it's not as if Nostradamus works down on the trading floor.

WHICH CAME FIRST: IMPLIED VOLATILITY OR THE EGG?

If you were to look at an option-pricing formula, you'd see variables like current stock price, strike price, days until expiration, interest rates, dividends and implied volatility, which are used to determine the option's price.

Market makers use implied volatility as an essential factor when determining what option prices should be. However, as we alluded to before, you can't calculate implied volatility without knowing the prices of options. So some traders experience a bit of "chicken or the egg" confusion about which comes first: implied volatility or option price.

In reality, it's not that difficult to understand. Usually, at-the-money option contracts are the most heavily traded in each expiration month. So market makers can allow supply and demand to set the at-the-money price for at-the-money options. Then, once the at-the-money option prices are determined, implied volatility is the only missing variable. So it's a matter of simple algebra to solve for it.

Once the implied volatility is determined for the at-the-money contracts in any given expiration month, market makers then use pricing models and advanced volatility skews to determine implied volatility at other strike prices that are less heavily traded. So you'll generally see variances

FIGURE 3: OPTION PRICING COMPONENTS

STOCK PRICE

STRIKE PRICE

EXPIRATION DATE

INTEREST RATE

DIVIDENDS

IMPLIED VOLATILITY

All this stuff gets entered into a pricing formula

= PRICE

Here is all the information you need to calculate an option's price. You can solve for any single component (like implied volatility) as long as you have all of the other data, including the price.

in implied volatility at different strike prices and expiration months.

But for now, let's stay focused on the implied volatility of the at-the-money option contract for the expiration month you're planning to trade. Because it's typically the most heavily traded contract, the at-the-money option will be the primary reflection of what the marketplace expects the underlying stock to do in the future.

However, watch out for odd events like mergers, acquisitions or rumors of bankruptcy. If any of these occur it can throw a wrench into the monkeyworks and seriously mess with the numbers.

USING IMPLIED VOLATILITY TO DETERMINE NEARER-TERM POTENTIAL STOCK MOVEMENTS

As mentioned above, implied volatility can help you gauge the probability that a stock will wind up at any given price at the end of a 12-month period. But now, you might be thinking, "That's all fine and dandy, but I don't usually trade 12-month options. How can implied volatility help my shorter-term trades?"

That's a great question. The most commonly traded options are in fact near-term, between 30 and 90 calendar days until expiration. So here's a quick and dirty formula you can use to calculate a one standard deviation move over the lifespan of your option contract – no matter the time frame.

$$\text{ONE STANDARD DEVIATION MOVE} = \frac{\text{STOCK PRICE} \times \text{IMPLIED VOLATILITY} \times \sqrt{\text{DAYS TO EXPIRATION}}}{\sqrt{365}}$$

As an example, let's use stock XYZ, still trading at $50 with implied volatility of 20%, 45 days from expiration.

$$\text{ONE STANDARD DEVIATION MOVE} = \frac{\$50 \times .20 \times \sqrt{45}}{\sqrt{365}}$$

$$\text{ONE STANDARD DEVIATION MOVE} = +/- 3.51$$

Remember: these quick and dirty calculations aren't 100% accurate, mainly because they assume a normal distribution instead of a log normal distribution (see sidebar). They're merely handy in grasping the concept of implied volatility and in getting a rough idea of the potential range of stock prices at expiration. For a more accurate calculation of what implied volatility is saying a stock might do, use TradeKing's **Probability Calculator**. *This tool will do the math for you using a log normal distribution assumption.*

THE THEORETICAL WORLD AND THE REAL WORLD

In order to be a successful option trader, you don't just need to be good at picking the direction a stock will move (or won't move), you also need to be good at predicting the timing of the move. Then, once you have made your forecasts, understanding implied volatility can help take the guesswork out of the potential price range on the stock.

It can't be emphasized enough, however, that implied volatility is what the marketplace expects the stock to do in theory. And as you probably know, the real world doesn't always operate in accordance with the theoretical world.

In the stock market crash of 1987, the market made a 20 standard deviation move. In theory, the odds of such a move are positively astronomical: about 1 in a gazillion. But in reality, it did happen. And not many traders saw it coming.

Although it's not always 100% accurate, implied volatility can be a useful tool. Because option trading is fairly difficult, we have to try to take advantage of every piece of information the market gives us.

A BRIEF ASIDE:

NORMAL DISTRIBUTION VS. LOG NORMAL DISTRIBUTION

All option pricing models assume "log normal distribution" whereas here, I'm using "normal distribution" for simplicity's sake.

As you know, a stock can only go down to zero, whereas it can theoretically go up to infinity. For example, it's conceivable a $20 stock can go up $30, but it can't go down $30. Downward movement has to stop when the stock reaches zero. Normal distribution does not account for this discrepancy; it assumes that the stock can move equally in either direction.

In a log normal distribution, on the other hand, a one standard deviation move to the upside may be larger than a one standard deviation move to the downside, especially as you move further out in time. That's because of the greater potential range on the upside than the downside.

Unless you're a real statistics geek, you probably wouldn't notice the difference. But as a result, the examples in this section aren't 100% accurate, so I feel it's necessary to point it out.

MEET THE GREEKS

(AT LEAST THE FOUR MOST IMPORTANT ONES)

Before you read the plays, it's a good idea to get to know these characters because they'll affect the price of every option you trade. Keep in mind as you're getting acquainted, the examples I use are "ideal world" examples. And as Plato would certainly tell you, in the real world things tend not to work quite as perfectly as they do in an ideal one.

DELTA

Beginning option traders sometimes assume that when a stock moves $1, the price of options based on that stock will move more than $1. That's a little silly when you really think about it. The option costs much less than the stock. Why should you be able to reap even more benefit than if you owned the stock?

It's important to have realistic expectations about the price behavior of the options you trade. So the real question is, how much will the price of an option move if the stock moves $1? That's where "delta" comes in.

Delta is the amount an option price is expected to move based on a $1 change in the underlying stock.

Calls have positive delta, between 0 and 1. That means if the stock price goes up and no other pricing variables change, the price for the call will

go up. Here's an example. If a call has a delta of .50 and the stock goes up $1, in theory, the price of the call will go up about $.50. If the stock goes down $1, in theory, the price of the call will go down about $.50.

Puts have a negative delta, between 0 and -1. That means if the stock goes up and no other pricing variables change, the price of the option will go down. For example, if a put has a delta of -.50 and the stock goes up $1, in theory, the price of the put will go down $.50. If the stock goes down $1, in theory, the price of the put will go up $.50.

As a general rule, in-the-money options will move more than out-of-the-money options, and short-term options will react more than longer-term options to the same price change in the stock.

As expiration nears, the delta for in-the-money calls will approach 1, reflecting a one-to-one reaction to price changes in the stock. Delta for out-of-the-money calls will approach 0 and won't react at all to price changes in the stock. That's because if they are held until expiration, calls will either be exercised and "become stock" or they will expire worthless and become nothing at all.

As expiration approaches, the delta for in-the-money puts will approach -1 and delta for out-of-the-money puts will approach 0. That's because if puts are held until expiration, the owner will either exercise the options and sell stock or the put will expire worthless.

NOTE: The Greeks represent the consensus of the marketplace as to how the option will react to changes in certain variables associated with the pricing of an option contract. There is no guarantee that these forecasts will be correct.

A DIFFERENT WAY TO THINK ABOUT DELTA

So far I've given you the textbook definition of delta. But here's another useful way to think about delta: the probability an option will wind up at least $.01 in-the-money at expiration.

Technically, this is not a valid definition because the actual math behind delta is not an advanced probability calculation. However, delta is frequently used synonymously with probability in the options world.

In casual conversation, it is customary to drop the decimal point in the delta figure, as in, "My option has a 60 delta." Or, "There is a 99 delta I am going to have a beer when I finish writing this section."

Usually, an at-the-money call option will have a delta of about .50, or "50 delta." That's because there should be a 50/50 chance the option winds up in- or out-of-the-money at expiration. Now let's look at how delta begins to change as an option gets further in- or out-of-the-money.

HOW STOCK PRICE MOVEMENT AFFECTS DELTA

As an option gets further in-the-money, the probability it will be in-the-money at expiration increases as well. So the option's delta will increase. As an option gets further out-of-the-money, the probability it will be in-the-money at expiration decreases. So the option's delta will decrease.

Imagine you own a call option on stock XYZ with a strike price of $50, and 60 days prior to expiration the stock price is exactly $50. Since it's an at-the-money option, the delta should be about .50. For sake of example, let's say the option is worth $2. So in theory, if the stock goes up to $51, the option price should go up from $2 to $2.50.

What, then, if the stock continues to go up from $51 to $52? There is now a higher probability that the option will end up in-the-money at expiration. So what will happen to delta? If you said, "Delta will increase," you're absolutely correct.

If the stock price goes up from $51 to $52, the option price might go up from $2.50 to $3.10. That's a $.60 move for a $1 movement in the stock. So delta has increased from .50 to .60 ($3.10 - $2.50 = $.60) as the stock got further in-the-money.

On the other hand, what if the stock drops from $50 to $49? The option price might go down from $2 to $1.50, again reflecting the .50 delta of at-the-money options ($2 - $1.50 = $.50). But if the stock keeps going down to $48, the option

might go down from $1.50 to $1.10. So delta in this case would have gone down to .40 ($1.50 - $1.10 = $.40). This decrease in delta reflects the lower probability the option will end up in-the-money at expiration.

HOW DELTA CHANGES AS EXPIRATION APPROACHES

Like stock price, time until expiration will affect the probability that options will finish in- or out-of-the-money. That's because as expiration approaches, the stock will have less time to move above or below the strike price for your option.

Because probabilities are changing as expiration approaches, delta will react differently to changes in the stock price. If calls are in-the-money just prior to expiration, the delta will approach 1 and the option will move penny-for-penny with the stock. In-the-money puts will approach -1 as expiration nears.

If options are out-of-the-money, they will approach 0 more rapidly than they would further out in time and stop reacting altogether to movement in the stock.

Imagine stock XYZ is at $50, with your $50 strike call option only one day from expiration. Again, the delta should be about .50, since there's theoretically a 50/50 chance of the stock moving in either direction. But what will happen if the stock goes up to $51?

Think about it. If there's only one day until expiration and the option is one point in-the-money, what's the probability the option will still be at least $.01 in-the-money by tomorrow? It's pretty high, right?

Of course it is. So delta will increase accordingly, making a dramatic move from .50 to about .90. Conversely, if stock XYZ drops from $50 to $49 just one day before the option expires, the delta might change from .50 to .10, reflecting the much lower probability that the option will finish in-the-money.

So as expiration approaches, changes in the stock value will cause more dramatic changes in delta, due to increased or decreased probability of finishing in-the-money.

REMEMBER THE TEXTBOOK DEFINITION OF DELTA, ALONG WITH THE ALAMO

I want to reiterate that the "textbook definition" of delta has nothing to do with the probability of options finishing in- or out-of-the-money. Again, delta is simply the amount an option price will move based on a $1 change in the underlying stock.

But looking at delta as the probability an option will finish in-the-money is a pretty nifty way to think about it. And if there's one thing I want to encourage in this playbook, it's nifty ways of thinking about options.

GAMMA

Gamma is the rate that delta will change based on a $1 change in the stock price. So if delta is the "speed" at which option prices change, you can think of gamma as the "acceleration." So options with the highest gamma are the most responsive to changes in the price of the underlying stock.

As I've mentioned, delta is a dynamic number that changes as the stock price changes. But delta doesn't change at the same rate for every option based on a given stock. Let's take another look at our call option on stock XYZ, with a strike price of $50, to see how gamma reflects the change in delta with respect to changes in stock price and time until expiration (Figure 1).

Note how delta and gamma change as the stock price moves up or down from $50 and the option moves in- or out-of-the-money. As you can see, the price of at-the-money options will change more significantly than the price of in- or out-of-the-money options with the same expiration. Also, the price of near-term at-the-money options will change more significantly than the price of longer-term at-the-money options.

Gamma Ray Gun

FIGURE 1: **DELTA AND GAMMA FOR STOCK XYZ CALL WITH $50 STRIKE PRICE**

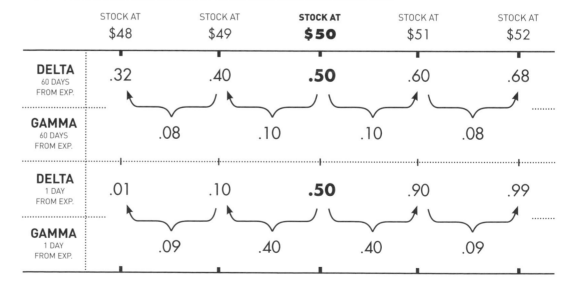

	STOCK AT $48	STOCK AT $49	**STOCK AT $50**	STOCK AT $51	STOCK AT $52
DELTA 60 DAYS FROM EXP.	.32	.40	**.50**	.60	.68
GAMMA 60 DAYS FROM EXP.		.08	.10	.10	.08
DELTA 1 DAY FROM EXP.	.01	.10	**.50**	.90	.99
GAMMA 1 DAY FROM EXP.		.09	.40	.40	.09

So what this talk about gamma boils down to is that the price of near-term at-the-money options will exhibit the most explosive response to price changes in the stock.

If you're an option buyer, high gamma is good as long as your forecast is correct. That's because as your option moves in-the-money, delta will approach 1 more rapidly. But if your forecast is wrong, it can come back to bite you by rapidly lowering your delta.

If you're an option seller and your forecast is incorrect, high gamma is the enemy. That's because it can cause your position to work against you at a more accelerated rate if the option you've sold moves in-the-money. But if your forecast is correct, high gamma is your friend since the value of the option you sold will lose value more rapidly.

THETA

Time decay is enemy number one for the option buyer. On the other hand, it's usually the option seller's best friend. Theta is the amount the price of calls and puts will decrease (at least in theory) for a one-day change in the time to expiration.

In the options market, the passage of time is similar to the effect of the hot summer sun on a block of ice. Each moment that passes causes some of the option's time value to "melt away." Furthermore, not only does the time value melt away, it does so at an accelerated rate as expiration approaches.

Check out figure 2. As you can see, an at-the-money 90-day option with a premium of $1.70 will lose $.30 of its value in one month. A 60-day option, on the other hand, might lose $.40 of its value over the course of the following month. And the 30-day option will lose the entire remaining $1 of time value by expiration.

At-the-money options will experience more significant dollar losses over time than in- or out-of-the-money options with the same underlying stock and expiration date. That's because at-the-money options have the most time value built into the premium. And the bigger the chunk of time value built into the price, the more there is to lose.

Keep in mind that for out-of-the-money options, theta will be lower than it is for at-the-money options. That's because the dollar amount of time value is smaller. However, the loss may be greater percentage-wise for out-of-the-money options because of the smaller time value.

When reading the plays, watch for the net effects of theta in the section called "As time goes by."

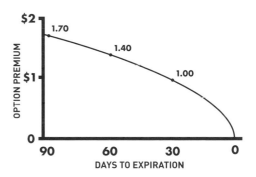

FIGURE 2: **TIME DECAY OF AN AT-THE-MONEY CALL OPTION**

This graph shows how an at-the-money option's value will decay over the last three months until expiration. Notice how time value melts away at an accelerated rate as expiration approaches.

VEGA

You can think of vega as the Greek who's a little shaky and over-caffeinated. It's the amount call and put prices will change, in theory, for a corresponding one-point change in implied volatility. Vega does not have any effect on the intrinsic value of options; it only affects the "time value" of an option's price.

Typically, as implied volatility increases, the value of options will increase. That's because an increase in implied volatility suggests an increased range of potential movement for the stock.

Let's examine a 30-day option on stock XYZ with a $50 strike price and the stock exactly at $50. Vega for this option might be .03. In other words, the value of the option might go up $.03 if implied volatility increases one point, and the value of the option might go down $.03 if implied volatility decreases one point.

Now, if you look at a 365-day at-the-money XYZ option, vega might be as high as .20. So the value of the option might change $.20 when implied volatility changes by a point (see figure 3).

FIGURE 3: VEGA FOR AT-THE-MONEY OPTIONS BASED ON STOCK XYZ

(XYZ = $50, STRIKE PRICE = $50)

TIME UNTIL EXP.	30 days	365 days
OPTION COST	$1.50	$5.36
VEGA	**.03**	**.20**

Obviously, as we go further out in time, there will be more time value built into the option contract. Since implied volatility only affects time value, longer-term options will have a higher vega than shorter-term options.

When reading the plays, watch for the effect of vega in the section called "Implied volatility."

WHERE'S RHO?

If you're a more advanced option trader, you might have noticed we're missing a Greek here. Namely, rho. That's the amount an option value will change in theory based on a one percentage-point change in interest rates.

Rho just stepped out for a gyro, since we don't talk about him that much in this playbook. Those of you who really get serious about options will eventually get to know this character far more intimately, but that's a subject for another book.

For now, just keep in mind that if you are trading shorter-term options, changing interest rates shouldn't affect the value of your options too much. But if you are trading longer-term options such as LEAPS, rho can have a much more significant effect due to greater "cost to carry."

CASHING OUT YOUR OPTIONS

The fact that option contracts can be opened or closed at any given point prior to expiration leads us to the mysterious and oft-misunderstood concept called "open interest."

OPTION OUTCOMES: CALENDAR YEAR 2008

Source: Options Clearing Corporation

So, you've bought or sold an option to open a "long" or "short" position. What now?

Some beginning option traders think that any time you buy or sell options, you eventually have to trade the underlying stock. That's simply not true. There are actually three things that can happen.

1) You can buy or sell to "close" the position prior to expiration.

2) The options expire out-of-the-money and worthless, so you do nothing.

3) The options expire in-the-money, usually resulting in a trade of the underlying stock if the option is exercised.

There's a common misconception that #2 is the most frequent outcome. Not so. Outcome #1 is actually the most frequent.

If you have a trade that's working in your favor, you can cash in by closing your position in the marketplace before the option expires. On the other hand, if you have a trade that's going against you, it's OK to cut and run. You don't necessarily have to wait until expiration to see what happens.

mmmm... pie.

- **11.6%** Exercised
- **19%** Expired worthless
- **69.4%** Bought or sold to close position

KEEPING TABS ON "OPEN INTEREST"

(OR: WHERE DO OPTIONS GO WHEN THEY DIE?)

As opposed to stocks, which have a fixed number of shares outstanding, there's no minimum or maximum number of option contracts that can exist for any given underlying stock. There will simply be as many option contracts as trader demand dictates.

Remember: whenever you trade an option contract, you might be creating a brand-new position (opening) or liquidating an existing one (closing). That's why whenever you enter an option order, it's not good enough to simply say "buy" or "sell" as you would with a stock. You need to specify whether you are buying or selling "to open" or "to close" your position.

In other words, options aren't necessarily hot potatoes that get passed around and wind up in someone's hands at expiration. Someone needs to look at the big picture and keep track of the overall number of outstanding option contracts in the marketplace. That's where The Options Clearing Corporation (OCC) comes in.

Every day, The OCC looks at the volume of options traded on any given stock, and they make note of how many options were marked "to open" versus "to close." And once they've tallied up the numbers, they can determine something called "open interest."

Simply put, open interest is the number of option contracts that exist for a particular stock. They can be tallied on as large a scale as all open contracts on a stock, or can be measured more specifically as option type (call or put) at a specific strike price with a specific expiration.

Obviously, if more of the volume on any given option is marked "to open" than "to close," open interest increases. Conversely, if more option trades are marked "to close" than "to open," open interest decreases.

FIGURE 1: **OPEN INTEREST**

XYZ=49.83

CALLS			PUTS	
VOLUME	OPEN INTEREST	STRIKE PRICE	VOLUME	OPEN INTEREST
0	12	**35**	10	361
304	139	**40**	10	971
62	2202	**45**	119	3568
191	6403	**50**	435	4246
195	2977	**55**	81	1141
36	173	**60**	22	643
5	15	**65**	0	19

Here's an example of trading volume and open interest figures for fictitious stock XYZ. Keep in mind that each option contract normally represents 100 shares of the stock.

This brings up a point worth noting: although you can keep track of trading volume on any given option throughout the day, open interest is a "lagging number." In other words, it is not updated during the course of a trading day. Instead, it is officially posted by The OCC the morning after any given trading session, once the figures have been calculated. For the rest of the trading day the figure remains static.

WHY OPEN INTEREST MATTERS TO YOU

As you can see from figure 1, open interest can vary from the call side to the put side, and from strike price to strike price.

High open interest for a given option contract means a lot of people are interested in that option. However, high open interest doesn't necessarily mean the people trading that contract have the correct forecast on the stock. After all, for every option buyer expecting one result, there's an option seller expecting something else to happen. So open interest doesn't necessarily indicate a bullish or bearish forecast.

The main benefit of trading options with high open interest is that it tends to reflect greater liquidity for that contract. So there will be less of a price discrepancy between what someone wants to pay for an option and how much someone wants to sell it for. Thus, there should be a higher likelihood your order will be filled at a price that's acceptable to you.

AND NOW, FOR A QUICK DISCLAIMER

It's very important to account for commissions, taxes, margin rates and other fees whenever you trade options because they can impact your bottom line. However, to make this book easier to read, I don't talk about them very much.

At any rate, TradeKing's commissions and fees are among the lowest in the business. So don't worry. We won't nickel and dime you. If we wanted to engage in chiseling, we would have become sculptors instead of brokers.

Just remember to factor all of the costs of each trade into your profit and loss calculations and consult your tax advisor whenever possible.

ROOKIES'

CORNER 🐷

GETTING
YOUR FEET WET
(WITHOUT GETTING IN
UP TO YOUR
YOU-KNOW-WHAT)

Option trading is more complicated than trading stock. And for a first-timer, it can be a little intimidating. That's why many investors decide to begin trading options by buying short-term calls. Especially out-of-the-money calls (strike price above the stock price), since they seem to follow a familiar pattern: buy low, sell high.

But for most investors, buying out-of-the-money short-term calls is probably not the best way to start trading options. Let's look at an example of why this is the case.

Imagine you're bullish on stock XYZ, trading at $50. As a beginning option trader, you might be tempted to buy calls 30 days from expiration with a strike price of $55, at a cost of $0.15, or $15 per contract. Why? Because you can buy a lot of them. Let's do the math. (And remember, one option contract usually equals 100 shares.)

Purchasing 100 shares of XYZ at $50 would cost $5000. But for the same $5000, you could buy 333 contracts of $55 calls, and control 33,300 shares. Holy smokes.

Imagine XYZ hits $56 within the next 30 days, and the $55 call trades at $1.05 just prior to expiration. You'd make $29,921.10 in a month ($34,965 sale price minus $4995 initially paid minus $48.90 TradeKing commissions). At first glance, that kind of leverage is very attractive indeed.

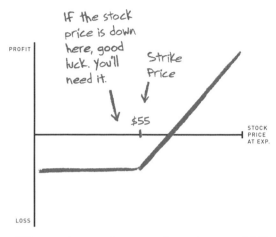

FIGURE 1: **CALL OPTION RISK PROFILE**

When you buy a call option with a strike price of $55 at a cost of $0.15, and the stock currently trading at $50, you need the stock price to rise $5.15 before your options expire in order to break even. That's a pretty significant rise in a short time. And that kind of move can be very difficult to predict.

ALL THAT GLITTERS ISN'T A GOLDEN OPTIONS TRADE

One of the problems with short-term out-of-the-money calls is that you not only have to be right about the direction the stock moves, but you also have to be right about the timing. That ratchets up the degree of difficulty.

Furthermore, to make a profit, the stock doesn't merely need to go past the strike price within a predetermined period of time. It needs to go past the strike price plus the cost of the option. In the case of the $55 call on stock XYZ, you'd need the stock to reach $55.15 within 30 days just to break even. And that doesn't even factor in commissions.

In essence, you're asking the stock to move more than 10% in less than a month. How many stocks are likely to do that? The answer you're looking for is, "Not many." In all probability, the stock won't reach the strike price, and the options will expire worthless. So in order to make money on an out-of-the-money call, you either need to outwit the market, or get plain lucky.

BEING CLOSE MEANS NO CIGAR

Imagine the stock rose to $54 during the 30 days of your option's lifetime. You were right about the direction the stock moved. But since you were wrong about how far it would go within a specific time frame, you'd lose your entire investment.

If you'd simply bought 100 shares of XYZ at $50, you'd be up $400 (minus TradeKing commission of $4.95). Even if your forecast was wrong and XYZ went down in price, it would most likely still be worth a significant portion of your initial investment. So the moral of the story is:

Don't get suckered in by the leverage you get from buying boatloads of short-term out-of-the-money calls.

HEY, DON'T GET ME WRONG

On the other hand, don't get the false impression that you should avoid calls altogether. In this book, I've outlined several ways to approach using them. In fact, this section outlines three plays for beginners to get their feet wet, and two of them do involve calls.

These plays are: A) writing covered calls, B) buying LEAPS calls (long-term options) as a stock substitute, and C) selling puts on a stock you want to buy.

The reason I chose these plays is because they're designed to enhance your stock portfolio. For now, rookies should aim for a balance between trading stocks and using options when you feel it's appropriate.

WRITING COVERED CALLS

Writing a covered call means you're selling someone else the right to purchase a stock that you already own, at a specific price, within a specified time frame. Because one option contract usually represents 100 shares, to run this play, you must own at least 100 shares for every call contract you plan to sell.

As a result of selling ("writing") the call, you'll pocket the premium right off the bat. The fact that you already own the stock means you're covered if the stock price rises past the strike price and the call options are assigned. You'll simply deliver stock you already own, reaping the additional benefit of the uptick on the stock.

HERE'S HOW YOU CAN WRITE YOUR FIRST COVERED CALL

First, choose a stock in your portfolio that has already performed fairly well, and which you are willing to sell if the call option is assigned. Avoid choosing a stock that you're very bullish on in the long-term. That way you won't feel too heartbroken if you do have to part with the stock and wind up missing out on further gains.

Now pick a strike price at which you'd be comfortable selling the stock. Normally, the strike price you choose should be out-of-the-money. That's because the goal is for the stock to rise further in price before you'll have to part with it.

Next, pick an expiration date for the option contract. Consider 30–45 days in the future as a starting point, but use your judgment. You want to look for a date that provides an acceptable premium for selling the call option at your chosen strike price.

As a general rule of thumb, some investors think about 2% of the stock value is an acceptable premium to look for. Remember, with options, time is money. The further you go out in time, the more an option will be worth. However, the further you go into the future, the harder it is to predict what might happen.

On the other hand, beware of receiving too much time value. If the premium seems abnormally high, there's usually a reason for it. Check for news in the marketplace that may affect the price of the stock, and remember if something seems too good to be true, it usually is.

OPTIONS GUY'S TIP:

☞ Try using the covered call chain on TradeKing.com to determine your optimal strike price and expiration date for the calls you plan to sell.

There are three possible outcomes for this play:

SCENARIO 1: THE STOCK GOES DOWN

If the stock price is down at the time the option expires, the good news is the call will expire worthless, and you'll keep the entire premium received for selling it. Obviously, the bad news is that the value of the stock is down. That's the nature of a covered call. The risk comes from owning the stock. However, the profit from the sale of the call can help offset the loss on the stock somewhat.

If the stock takes a dive prior to the expiration date of the call, don't panic. You're not locked into your position. Although losses will be accruing on the stock, the call option you sold will go down in value as well. That's a good thing because it will be possible to buy the call back for less money than you received to sell it. If your opinion on the stock has changed, you can simply close your position by buying back the call contract, and then dump the stock.

SCENARIO 2: THE STOCK STAYS THE SAME OR GOES UP A LITTLE, BUT DOESN'T REACH THE STRIKE PRICE

There's really no bad news in this scenario. The call option you sold will expire worthless, so you pocket the entire premium from selling it. Perhaps you've seen some gains on the underlying stock, which you will still own. You can't complain about that.

SCENARIO 3: THE STOCK RISES ABOVE THE STRIKE PRICE

If the stock is above the strike price at expiration, the call option will be assigned and you'll have to sell 100 shares of the stock.

If the stock skyrockets after you sell the shares, you might consider kicking yourself for missing out on any additional gains, but don't. You made a conscious decision that you were willing to part with the stock at the strike price, and you achieved the maximum profit potential from the play.

Pat yourself on the back. Or if you're not very flexible, have somebody else pat your back for you. You've done well.

THE RECAP ON THE LOGIC

Many investors use a covered call as a first foray into option trading. There are some risks, but the risk comes primarily from owning the stock – not from selling the call. The sale of the option only limits opportunity on the upside.

When running a covered call, you're taking advantage of time decay on the options you sold. Every day the stock doesn't move, the call you sold will decline in value, which benefits you as the seller. (Time decay is an important concept. So as a beginner, it's good for you to see it in action.)

As long as the stock price doesn't reach the strike price, your stock won't get called away. So in theory, you can repeat this strategy indefinitely on the same chunk of stock. And with every covered call you run, you'll become more familiar with the workings of the option market.

You may also appear smarter to yourself when you look in the mirror. But I'm not making any promises about that.

this can be painful

usually painless (unless there is sunburn involved)

BUYING LEAPS CALLS AS A STOCK SUBSTITUTE

I've already warned you against starting off by purchasing out-of-the-money short-term calls. Here's a method of using calls that might work for the beginning option trader: buying long-term calls, or "LEAPS."

The goal here is to reap benefits similar to those you'd see if you owned the stock, while limiting the risks you'd face by having the stock in your portfolio. In effect, your LEAPS call acts as a "stock substitute."

WHAT ARE LEAPS?

LEAPS are longer-term options. The term stands for "Long-term Equity AnticiPation Securities," in case you're the kind of person who wonders about that sort of thing. And no, that capital P in AnticiPation wasn't a typo, in case you're the kind of person who wonders about that sort of thing too.

Options with more than 9 months until expiration are considered LEAPS. They behave just like other options, so don't let the term confuse you. It simply means that they have a long shelf-life.

LET'S GET STARTED

First, choose a stock. You should use exactly the same process you would use if purchasing the stock. Go to TradeKing's Quotes + Research menu, and analyze the stock's fundamentals to make sure you like it.

Now, you need to pick your strike price. You want to buy a LEAPS call that is deep in-the-money. (When talking about a call, "in-the-money" means the strike price is below the current stock price.) A general rule of thumb to use while running this play is to look for a delta of .80 or more at the strike price you choose.

Remember, a delta of .80 means that if the stock rises $1, then in theory, the price of your option will rise $0.80. If delta is .90, then if the stock rises $1, in theory your options will rise $0.90, and so forth. The delta at each strike price will be displayed on TradeKing's option chains.

As a starting point, consider a LEAPS call that is at least 20% of the stock price in-the-money. (For example, if the underlying stock costs $100, buy a call with a strike price of $80 or lower.) However, for particularly volatile stocks, you may need to go deeper in-the-money to get the delta you're looking for.

The deeper in-the-money you go, the more expensive your option will be. That's because it will have more "intrinsic value." But the benefit is that it will also have a higher delta. And the higher your delta, the more your option will behave as a stock substitute.

THE CAVEAT

You must keep in mind that even long-term options have an expiration date. If the stock shoots skyward the day after your option expires, it does you no good. Furthermore, as expiration approaches, options lose their value at an accelerating rate. So pick your time frame carefully.

As a general rule of thumb, consider buying a call that won't expire for at least a year or more. That makes this play a fine strategy for the longer-term investor. After all, we're treating this strategy as an investment, not pure speculation.

PICK A NUMBER

Now that you've chosen your strike price and month of expiration, you need to decide how many LEAPS calls to buy. As we say so many times in this book, you should usually trade the same quantity of options as the number of shares you're accustomed to trading. Pardon me for being redundant, but that's important.

If you'd typically buy 100 shares, buy one call. If you'd typically buy 200 shares, buy two calls, and so on. Don't go too crazy, because if your call options finish out-of-the-money, you may lose your entire investment.

HURRY UP AND WAIT

Now that you've purchased your LEAPS call(s), it's time to play the waiting game. Just like when you're trading stocks, you need to have a predefined price at which you'll be satisfied with your option gains, and get out of your position. You also need a predefined stop-loss if the price of your option(s) go down sharply.

Trading psychology is a big part of being a successful option investor. Be consistent. Stick to your guns. Don't panic. And don't get too greedy.

SELLING CASH-SECURED PUTS ON STOCK YOU WANT TO BUY

What if you could buy stocks for less than the current market price? And what if you could make money when you're wrong about the direction of the market? If either of those scenarios sounds appealing to you, then perhaps you should consider selling a cash-secured put.

WHEN TO RUN THIS PLAY

You're long-term bullish on a stock, but you don't want to pay the current market price for it. In other words, if the stock dips, you wouldn't mind buying it. You might consider entering a limit order at the price you'd like to pay for the shares. But selling a cash-secured put gives you another method of buying the stock below the current market price, with the added benefit of receiving the premium from the sale of the put.

HOW TO DO IT

Sell an out-of-the-money put (strike price below the stock price). You may want to consider choosing the first strike price below the current trading price for the stock, because that will increase the probability the put will be assigned, and you'll wind up acquiring the stock.

In order to receive a desirable premium, a time frame to shoot for when selling the put is anywhere from 30–45 days from expiration. This will enable you to take advantage of accelerating time decay on the option's price as expiration approaches, and hopefully provide enough premium to be worth your while. But what you consider a good return is up to you.

Once you've chosen your strike price and month of expiration, you'll need to make sure there's enough cash in your account to pay for the shares if the put is assigned (hence the term "cash-secured" puts).

Ideally, you want the stock price to dip slightly below the strike price, and stay there until expiration. That way, the buyer of your put will exercise it, you will be assigned, and you'll be obligated to buy the stock. The premium received from selling the put can be applied to the cost of the shares, ultimately lowering the cost basis of the stock purchase.

LET'S LOOK AT SOME EXAMPLES OF WHAT MIGHT HAPPEN

Imagine stock XYZ is trading at $52 per share, but you want to pay less than $50 per share for 100 shares. You sell one put contract with a strike price of $50, 45 days prior to expiration, and receive a premium of $1. Since one contract usually equals 100 shares, you receive $94.40 ($100 minus $5.60 commission).

If the put is assigned, you'll be obligated to buy 100 shares of XYZ at $50. In order to be cash-secured, you'll need at least $5000 in your account. Since you've already received $94.40 from the sale of the put, you only need to come up with $4905.60 ($5000 minus $94.40).

How might this trade pan out? Let's examine four possible outcomes.

SCENARIO 1: THE STOCK DIPS SLIGHTLY BELOW $50

This is a great scenario. Let's say the stock is at $49.75 at expiration. The put will be assigned, and you will buy 100 shares at $50 per share. However, since you already received a $1 per share premium for the sale of the put, it's as if you paid net $49 per share. Since the stock is currently trading for $49.75, you achieved a savings of $64.45 ($0.75 x 100 shares - $10.55 commission). Huzzah.

SCENARIO 2: THE STOCK RISES

Now imagine the stock rises, and ends up at $54 at expiration. That means there's some bad news, but there's some good news too. The bad news is you were wrong about the short-term movement of the stock. Since it didn't come down to the strike price, the put won't be assigned and you won't get the stock at $50 per share. If you had simply bought the stock at $52 instead of selling the put, you would have already made $2 per share: double the $1 premium you received.

On the other hand, you did receive a $1 premium, or $94.40 ($100 minus $5.60 commission) for being wrong. And there's nothing wrong with that. Plus, the cash you used to secure your put will be available to you for other trades. So there's a silver lining to this otherwise cloudy trade.

SCENARIO 3: THE STOCK DIPS SLIGHTLY FURTHER THAN YOU ANTICIPATED

What if the stock is at $48 as the options expire? The put will be assigned and you will pay $50 per share. Subtracting the $1 put premium received and commissions paid ($10.55), it is as if you paid just over $49 per share. You may be tempted to curse and think you overpaid for the stock by $1 per share.

But look at the bright side. If you hadn't used this strategy, you might've simply entered a limit order at $50 and not even received the put premium. That would be worse, right? Plus, now that you own the stock, it might make a rebound. Let's hope you're a good long-term stock picker.

SCENARIO 4: THE STOCK COMPLETELY TANKS

This is obviously the worst-case scenario. Let's hope your forecasting would never be this wrong. But what if the stock does completely tank? There are a couple of things you can do.

First, you can accept assignment and pay $50 per share, irrespective of current stock price. In this case, you'd be hoping your long-term forecast is correct, and the stock will bounce back significantly.

If you doubt the stock will make a recovery, your other choice is to close your position prior to expiration. That will remove any obligation you have to buy the stock. To close your position, simply buy back the 50-strike put. Keep in mind, the further the stock price goes down, the more expensive that will be.

This scenario demonstrates the importance of having a stop-loss plan in place. If the stock goes beneath the lowest point where you're comfortable buying it, a stop order should be placed to buy back the 50-strike put. This is much the same concept as a stop order you might have on stocks in your portfolio.

THE RECAP ON THE LOGIC

Selling cash-secured puts is a substitute for placing a limit order on a stock you wish to own. You receive a premium for selling the puts, and if the options are assigned, the premium can be applied to the purchase of the stock.

If the stock doesn't dip below the strike price by expiration, the puts will probably not be assigned, and you won't have the opportunity to buy the stock at the strike price. However, the options will expire worthless and you'll get to keep the premium. And that's a good thing.

Just remember, only sell puts on the number of shares you can reasonably afford to buy. And have a stop-loss plan in place, in case the stock goes completely in the tank.

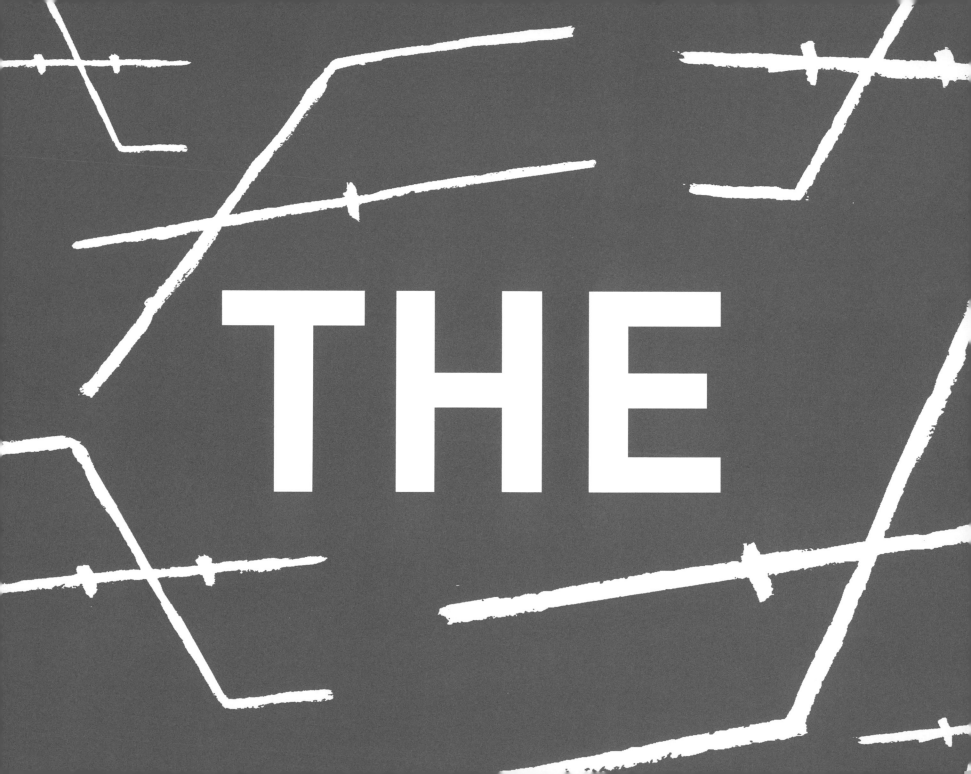

WHERE TO FIND YOUR FAVORITE PLAYS

KEY TO INTERPRETING SYMBOLS

🐂 » BULLISH

🐻 » BEARISH

Ⓝ » NEUTRAL

❓ » NOT SURE - You think the stock is going someplace, but you don't know which direction.

ONE-LEG PLAYS

PLAY ONE
LONG CALL » P40 🐂

PLAY TWO
LONG PUT » P42 🐻

PLAY THREE
SHORT CALL » P44 🐻 Ⓝ

PLAY FOUR
SHORT PUT » P46 🐂 Ⓝ

PLAY FIVE
CASH-SECURED PUT » P48 🐻 🐂

PLAYS INVOLVING A STOCK POSITION

PLAY SIX
COVERED CALL » P50 Ⓝ 🐂

PLAY SEVEN
PROTECTIVE PUT » P52 🐂

PLAY EIGHT
COLLAR » P54 🐂 ❓

TWO-LEG PLAYS

PLAY NINE
FIG LEAF » P56 🐂

PLAY TEN
LONG CALL SPREAD » P60 🐂

PLAY ELEVEN
LONG PUT SPREAD » P62 🐻

PLAY TWELVE
SHORT CALL SPREAD » P64 🐻 Ⓝ

PLAY THIRTEEN
SHORT PUT SPREAD » P66 🐂 Ⓝ

PLAY FOURTEEN
LONG STRADDLE » P68 ❓

PLAY FIFTEEN
SHORT STRADDLE » P70 Ⓝ

PLAY SIXTEEN
LONG STRANGLE » P72 ❓

PLAY SEVENTEEN
SHORT STRANGLE » P74 Ⓝ

PLAY EIGHTEEN
LONG COMBINATION » P76 🐂

PLAY NINETEEN
SHORT COMBINATION » P78 🐻

Keep in mind that multi-leg strategies are subject to additional risks and multiple commissions and may be subject to particular tax consequences. Please consult with your tax advisor prior to engaging in these strategies.

LONG CALL

THE SETUP

• Buy a call, strike price A

• Generally, the stock price will be at or above strike A

WHO SHOULD RUN IT

Veterans and higher

NOTE: Many rookies begin trading options by purchasing out-of-the-money short-term calls. That's because they tend to be cheap, and you can buy a lot of them. However, they're probably not the best way to get your feet wet. See the "Rookies' Corner" section of this book for other plays to consider.

WHEN TO RUN IT

 You're bullish as a matador.

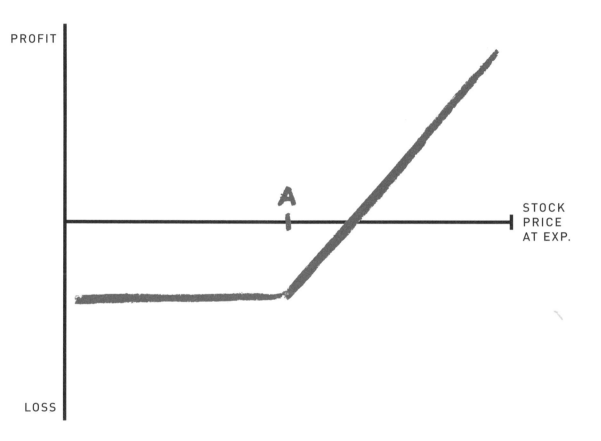

THE STRATEGY

A long call gives you the right to buy the underlying stock at strike price A.

Calls may be used as an alternative to buying stock outright. You can profit if the stock rises, without taking on all of the downside risk that would result from owning the stock. It is also possible to gain leverage over a greater number of shares than you could afford to buy outright because calls are always less expensive than the stock itself.

But be careful, especially with short-term out-of-the-money calls. If you buy too many option contracts, you are actually increasing your risk. Options may expire worthless and you can lose your entire investment, whereas if you own the stock it will usually still be worth something. (Except for certain banking stocks that shall remain nameless.)

OPTIONS GUY'S TIPS:

☞ Don't go overboard with the leverage you can get when buying calls. A general rule of thumb is this: If you're used to buying 100 shares of stock per trade, buy one option contract (1 contract = 100 shares). If you're comfortable buying 200 shares, buy two option contracts, and so on.

☞ If you do purchase a call, you may wish to consider buying the contract in-the-money, since it's likely to have a larger delta (that is, changes in the option's value will correspond more closely with any change in the stock price). Try looking for a delta of .80 or greater if possible. In-the-money options are more expensive because they have intrinsic value, but you get what you pay for.

BREAK-EVEN AT EXPIRATION

Strike A plus the cost of the call.

THE SWEET SPOT

The stock goes through the roof.

MAXIMUM POTENTIAL PROFIT

There's a theoretically unlimited profit potential, if the stock goes to infinity. (Please note: I've never actually seen a stock go to infinity. Sorry.)

MAXIMUM POTENTIAL LOSS

Risk is limited to the premium paid for the call option.

MARGIN REQUIREMENT

After the trade is paid for, no additional margin is required.

AS TIME GOES BY

For this play, time decay is the enemy. It will negatively affect the value of the option you bought.

IMPLIED VOLATILITY

After the play is established, you want implied volatility to increase. It will increase the value of the option you bought, and also reflects an increased possibility of a price swing without regard for direction (but you'll hope the direction is up).

CHECK YOUR PLAY WITH TRADEKING TOOLS

• Use the *Profit + Loss Calculator* to establish break-even points, evaluate how your strategy might change as expiration approaches, and analyze the Greeks.

• Remember: if out-of-the-money options are cheap, they're usually cheap for a reason. Use the *Probability Calculator* to help you form an opinion on your option's chances of expiring in-the-money.

• Use the *Technical Analysis Tool* to look for bullish indicators.

LONG PUT

THE SETUP

• Buy a put, strike price A

• Generally, the stock price will be at or below strike A

WHO SHOULD RUN IT

Veterans and higher

WHEN TO RUN IT

 You're bearish as a grizzly.

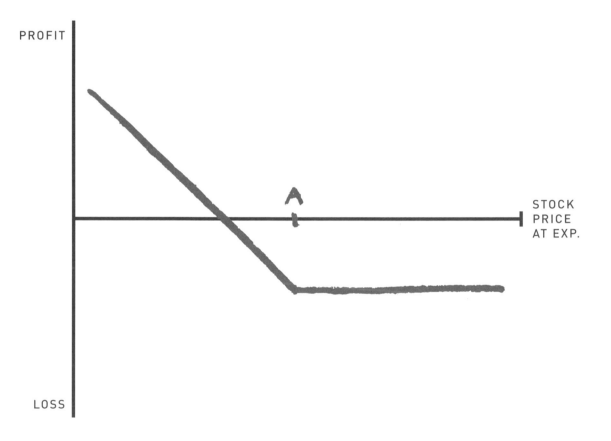

THE STRATEGY

A long put gives you the right to sell the underlying stock at strike price A.

If there were no such thing as puts, the only way to benefit from a downward movement in the market would be to sell stock short. The problem with shorting stock is you're exposed to theoretically unlimited risk if the stock price rises.

But when you use puts as an alternative to short stock, your risk is limited to the cost of the option contracts. If the stock goes up (the worst-case scenario) you don't have to deliver shares as you would with short stock. You simply allow your puts to expire worthless or sell them to close your position (if they're still worth anything).

But be careful, especially with short-term out-of-the-money puts. If you buy too many option contracts, you are actually increasing your risk. Options may expire worthless and you can lose your entire investment.

Puts can also be used to help protect the value of stocks you already own. These are called "protective puts." See Play Seven.

OPTIONS GUY'S TIPS:

☞ Don't go overboard with the leverage you can get when buying puts. A general rule of thumb is this: If you're used to selling 100 shares of stock short per trade, buy one put contract (1 contract = 100 shares). If you're comfortable selling 200 shares short, buy two put contracts, and so on.

☞ You may wish to consider buying an in-the-money put, since it's likely to have a greater delta (that is, changes in the option's value will correspond more closely with any change in the stock price). Try looking for a delta of -.80 or greater if possible. In-the-money options are more expensive because they have intrinsic value, but you get what you pay for.

BREAK-EVEN AT EXPIRATION

Strike A minus the cost of the put.

THE SWEET SPOT

The stock goes right in the tank.

MAXIMUM POTENTIAL PROFIT

There's a substantial profit potential. If the stock goes to zero you make the entire strike price minus the cost of the put contract. Keep in mind, however, stocks usually don't go to zero. So be realistic, and don't plan on buying an Italian sports car after just one trade.

MAXIMUM POTENTIAL LOSS

Risk is limited to the premium paid for the put.

MARGIN REQUIREMENT

After the trade is paid for, no additional margin is required.

AS TIME GOES BY

For this play, time decay is the enemy. It will negatively affect the value of the option you bought.

IMPLIED VOLATILITY

After the play is established, you want implied volatility to increase. It will increase the value of the option you bought, and also reflects an increased possibility of a price swing without regard for direction (but you'll hope the direction is down).

CHECK YOUR PLAY WITH TRADEKING TOOLS

• Use the **Profit + Loss Calculator** to establish break-even points, evaluate how your strategy might change as expiration approaches, and analyze the Greeks.

• Remember: if out-of-the-money options are cheap, they're usually cheap for a reason. Use the **Probability Calculator** to help you form an opinion on your option's chances of expiring in-the-money.

• Use the **Technical Analysis Tool** to look for bearish indicators.

SHORT
CALL

AKA Naked Call; Uncovered Call

THE SETUP

- Sell a call, strike price A
- Generally, the stock price will be below strike A

WHO SHOULD RUN IT

All-Stars only

NOTE: Uncovered short calls (selling a call on a stock you don't own) is only suited for the most advanced option traders. It is not a play for the faint of heart.

WHEN TO RUN IT

  You're bearish to neutral.

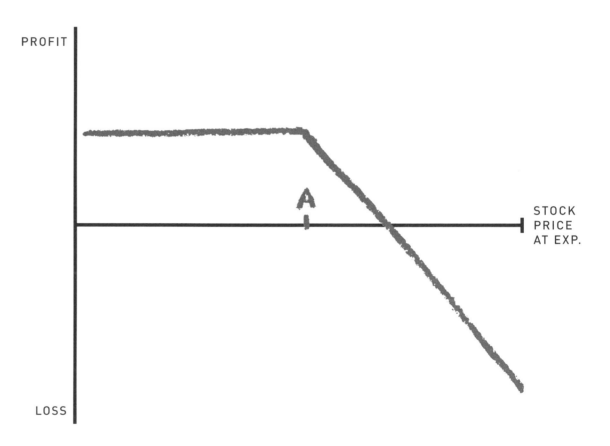

THE STRATEGY

Selling the call obligates you to sell stock at strike price A if the option is assigned.

When running this play, you want the call you sell to expire worthless. That's why most investors sell out-of-the-money options.

This play has a low profit potential if the stock remains below strike A at expiration, but unlimited potential risk if the stock goes up. The reason some traders run this play is that there is a high probability for success when selling very out-of-the-money options. If the market moves against you, then you must have a stop-loss plan in place. Keep a watchful eye on this play as it unfolds.

👤 OPTIONS GUY'S TIPS:

☞ You may wish to consider ensuring that strike A is around one standard deviation out-of-the-money at initiation. That will increase your probability of success. However, the higher the strike price, the lower the premium received from this play.

☞ Some investors may wish to run this play using index options rather than options on individual stocks. That's because historically, indexes have not been as volatile as individual stocks. Fluctuations in an index's component stock prices tend to cancel one another out, lessening the volatility of the index as a whole.

⓪ BREAK-EVEN AT EXPIRATION

Strike A plus the premium received for the call.

💲 THE SWEET SPOT

There's a large sweet spot. As long as the stock price is at or below strike A at expiration, you make your maximum profit. That's why this strategy is enticing to some traders.

⬆ MAXIMUM POTENTIAL PROFIT

Potential profit is limited to the premium received for selling the call.

⬇ MAXIMUM POTENTIAL LOSS

Risk is theoretically unlimited. If the stock keeps rising above strike A, you keep losing money. You may lose some hair as well. So hold onto your hat and stick to your stop-loss if the trade doesn't go your way.

% MARGIN REQUIREMENT

See Appendix A for margin requirement.

⏱ AS TIME GOES BY

For this play, time decay is your friend. You want the price of the option you sold to approach zero. That means if you choose to close your position prior to expiration, it will be less expensive to buy it back.

✦ IMPLIED VOLATILITY

After the play is established, you want implied volatility to decrease. That will decrease the price of the option you sold, so if you choose to close your position prior to expiration it will be less expensive to do so.

✔ CHECK YOUR PLAY WITH TRADEKING TOOLS

• Use the *Profit + Loss Calculator* to establish break-even points, evaluate how your strategy might change as expiration approaches, and analyze the Greeks.

• Use the *Probability Calculator* to verify that the call you sell is about one standard deviation out-of-the-money.

• Use the *Technical Analysis Tool* to look for bearish indicators.

SHORT PUT

AKA Naked Put; Uncovered Put

THE SETUP

- Sell a put, strike price A
- Generally, the stock price will be above strike A

WHO SHOULD RUN IT

All-Stars only

NOTE: Selling puts as pure speculation, with no intention of buying the stock, is suited only to the most advanced option traders. It is not a play for the faint of heart.

WHEN TO RUN IT

 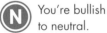 You're bullish to neutral.

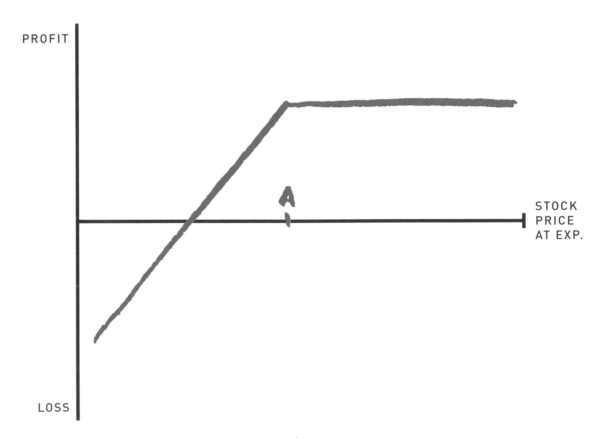

THE STRATEGY

Selling the put obligates you to buy stock at strike price A if the option is assigned.

When selling puts with no intention of buying the stock, you want the puts you sell to expire worthless. This play has a low profit potential if the stock remains above strike A at expiration, but substantial potential risk if the stock goes down. The reason some traders run this play is that there is a high probability for success when selling very out-of-the-money puts. If the market moves against you, then you must have a stop-loss plan in place. Keep a watchful eye on this play as it unfolds.

OPTIONS GUY'S TIPS:

☞ You may wish to consider ensuring that strike A is around one standard deviation out-of-the-money at initiation. That will increase your probability of success. However, the lower the strike price, the lower the premium received from this play.

☞ Some investors may wish to run this play using index options rather than options on individual stocks. That's because historically, indexes have not been as volatile as individual stocks. Fluctuations in an index's component stock prices tend to cancel one another out, lessening the volatility of the index as a whole.

BREAK-EVEN AT EXPIRATION

Strike A minus the premium received for the put.

THE SWEET SPOT

There's a large sweet spot. As long as the stock price is at or above strike A at expiration, you make your maximum profit. That's why this strategy is enticing to some traders.

MAXIMUM POTENTIAL PROFIT

Potential profit is limited to the premium received for selling the put.

MAXIMUM POTENTIAL LOSS

Potential loss is substantial, but limited to the strike price minus the premium received if the stock goes to zero.

MARGIN REQUIREMENT

See Appendix A for margin requirement.

AS TIME GOES BY

For this play, time decay is your friend. You want the price of the option you sold to approach zero. That means if you choose to close your position prior to expiration, it will be less expensive to buy it back.

IMPLIED VOLATILITY

After the play is established, you want implied volatility to decrease. That will decrease the price of the option you sold, so if you choose to close your position prior to expiration it will be less expensive to do so.

CHECK YOUR PLAY WITH TRADEKING TOOLS

• Use the *Profit + Loss Calculator* to establish break-even points, evaluate how your strategy might change as expiration approaches, and analyze the Greeks.

• Use the *Probability Calculator* to verify that the put you sell is about one standard deviation out-of-the-money.

• Use the *Technical Analysis Tool* to look for bullish indicators.

CASH-SECURED PUT

THE SETUP

- Sell a put, strike price A

- Keep enough cash on hand to buy the stock if the put is assigned

- Generally, the stock price will be above strike A

WHO SHOULD RUN IT

Rookies and higher

NOTE: Cash-secured puts can be executed by investors at any level. See the "Rookies' Corner" for a more in-depth explanation of this play.

WHEN TO RUN IT

  You're slightly bearish short-term; bullish long-term.

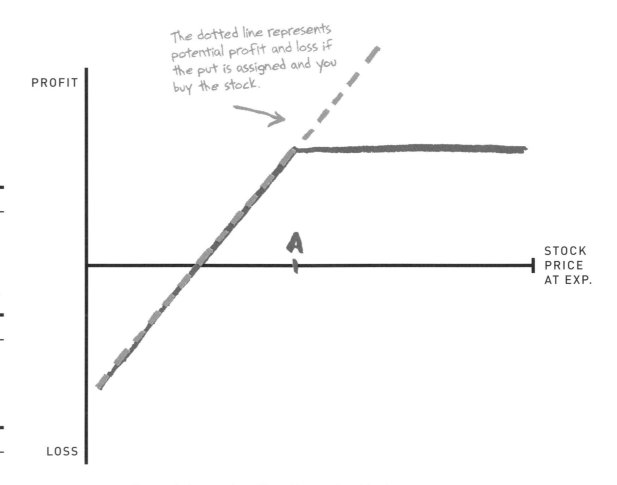

The dotted line represents potential profit and loss if the put is assigned and you buy the stock.

PROFIT

LOSS

A

STOCK PRICE AT EXP.

NOTE: This graph shows profit and loss of long stock and the short put.

THE STRATEGY

Selling the put obligates you to buy stock at strike price A if the option is assigned.

In this instance, you're selling the put with the intention of buying the stock after the put is assigned. When running this play, you may wish to consider selling the put slightly out-of-the-money. If you do so, you're hoping that the stock will make a bearish move, dip below the strike price, and stay there. That way the put will be assigned and you'll end up owning the stock. Naturally, you'll want the stock to rise in the long-term.

The premium received for the put you sell will lower the cost basis on the stock you want to buy. If the stock doesn't make a bearish move by expiration, you still keep the premium for selling the put. That's sort of nice, because it's one of the few instances when you can profit by being wrong.

👤 OPTIONS GUY'S TIP:

☞ Don't go overboard with the leverage you can get when selling puts. A general rule of thumb is this: If you're used to buying 100 shares of stock per trade, sell one put contract (1 contract = 100 shares). If you're comfortable buying 200 shares short, sell two put contracts, and so on.

⑩ BREAK-EVEN AT EXPIRATION

Strike A minus the premium received for the put.

💲 THE SWEET SPOT

You want the stock price to be just below strike A at expiration. Remember, the goal here is to wind up owning the stock.

⬆ MAXIMUM POTENTIAL PROFIT

Potential profit is limited to the premium received from selling the put. (If the puts are assigned, potential profit is changed to a "long stock" position.)

⬇ MAXIMUM POTENTIAL LOSS

Potential loss is substantial, but limited to the strike price if the stock goes to zero. (If the puts are assigned, potential loss is changed to a "long stock" position.)

％ MARGIN REQUIREMENT

See Appendix A for margin requirement.

⌚ AS TIME GOES BY

For this play, time decay is your friend. You want the price of the option you sold to approach zero. That means if you choose to close your position prior to expiration, it will be less expensive to buy it back.

⟳ IMPLIED VOLATILITY

After the play is established, you want implied volatility to decrease. That will decrease the price of the option you sold, so if you choose to close your position prior to expiration it will be less expensive to do so.

✓ CHECK YOUR PLAY WITH TRADEKING TOOLS

• Use the **Profit + Loss Calculator** to establish break-even points, evaluate how your strategy might change as expiration approaches, and analyze the Greeks.

• Look at stock fundamentals on TradeKing's research page. The idea is to hold the stock longer-term, so you need to be comfortable with that.

COVERED CALL

THE SETUP

• You own the stock

• Sell a call, strike price A

• Generally, the stock price will be below strike A

WHO SHOULD RUN IT

Rookies and higher

NOTE: Covered calls can be executed by investors at any level. See the "Rookies' Corner" for a more in-depth explanation of this play.

WHEN TO RUN IT

  You're neutral to bullish, and you're willing to sell stock if it reaches a specific price.

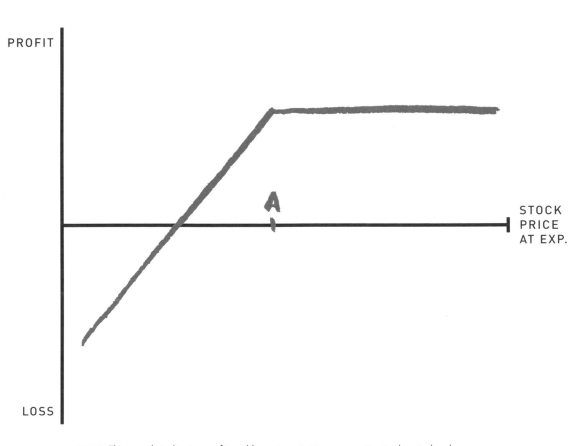

NOTE: This graph indicates profit and loss at expiration, respective to the stock value when you sold the call.

THE STRATEGY

Selling the call obligates you to sell stock you already own at strike price A if the option is assigned.

Some investors will run this play after they've already seen nice gains on the stock. Often, they will sell out-of-the-money calls, so if the stock price goes up, they're willing to part with the stock and take the profit.

Covered calls can also be used to achieve income on the stock above and beyond any dividends. The goal in that case is for the options to expire worthless.

If you buy the stock and sell the calls all at the same time, it's called a "Buy / Write." Some investors use a Buy / Write as a way to lower the cost basis of a stock they've just purchased.

👤 OPTIONS GUY'S TIPS:

☞ As a general rule of thumb, you may wish to consider running this play approximately 30–45 days from expiration to take advantage of accelerating time decay as expiration approaches. Of course, this depends on the underlying stock and market conditions such as implied volatility.

☞ You may wish to consider selling the call with a premium that represents at least 2% of the current stock price (premium ÷ stock price). But ultimately, it's up to you what premium will make running this play worth your while.

☞ Beware of receiving too much time value. If the premium seems abnormally high, there's usually a reason for it. Check for news in the marketplace that may affect the price of the stock. Remember, if something seems too good to be true, it usually is.

⊙ BREAK-EVEN AT EXPIRATION

Current stock price minus the premium received for selling the call.

$ THE SWEET SPOT

The sweet spot for this strategy depends on your objective. If you are selling covered calls to earn income on your stock, then you want the stock to remain as close to the strike price as possible without going above it.

If you want to sell the stock while making additional profit by selling the calls, then you want the stock to rise above the strike price and stay there at expiration. That way, the calls will be assigned.

However, you probably don't want the stock to shoot too high, or you might be a bit disappointed that you parted with it. But don't fret if that happens. You still made out all right on the stock. Do yourself a favor and stop getting quotes on it.

⬆ MAXIMUM POTENTIAL PROFIT

When the call is first sold, potential profit is limited to the strike price minus the current stock price plus the premium received for selling the call.

⬇ MAXIMUM POTENTIAL LOSS

You receive a premium for selling the option, but most downside risk comes from owning the stock, which may potentially lose its value. However, selling the option does create an "opportunity risk." That is, if the stock price skyrockets, the calls might be assigned and you'll miss out on those gains.

% MARGIN REQUIREMENT

Because you own the stock, no additional margin is required.

❈ AS TIME GOES BY

For this play, time decay is your friend. You want the price of the option you sold to approach zero. That means if you choose to close your position prior to expiration, it will be less expensive to buy it back.

✦ IMPLIED VOLATILITY

After the play is established, you want implied volatility to decrease. That will decrease the price of the option you sold, so if you choose to close your position prior to expiration it will be less expensive to do so.

✓ CHECK YOUR PLAY WITH TRADEKING TOOLS

• Use the *Profit + Loss Calculator* to establish break-even points, evaluate how your strategy might change as expiration approaches, and analyze the Greeks.

• View the *Option Chains* for your stock. Select the covered call option chain, and review the "Static Return" and "If Called Return" columns to make sure you're happy with potential outcomes. Static Return assumes the stock price is unchanged at expiration and the call expires worthless. If Called Return assumes the stock price rises above the strike price and the call is assigned.

PROTECTIVE PUT

THE SETUP

- You own the stock

- Buy a put, strike price A

- Generally, the stock price will be above strike A

WHO SHOULD RUN IT

Rookies and higher

WHEN TO RUN IT

 You're bullish but nervous.

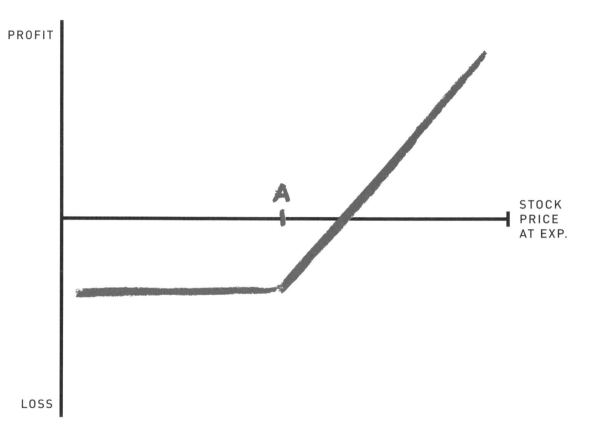

NOTE: This graph indicates profit and loss at expiration, respective to the stock value when you bought the put.

THE STRATEGY

Purchasing a protective put gives you the right to sell stock you already own at strike price A.

Protective puts are handy when your outlook is bullish but you want to protect the value of stocks in your portfolio in the event of a downturn. They can also help you cut back on your antacid intake in times of market uncertainty.

Protective puts are often used as an alternative to stop orders. The problem with stop orders is they sometimes work when you don't want them to work, and when you really need them they don't work at all. For example, if a stock's price is fluctuating but not really tanking, a stop order might get you out prematurely. If that happens, you probably won't be too happy if the stock bounces back. Or, if a major news event happens overnight and the stock gaps down significantly on the open, you might not get out at your stop price. Instead, you'll get out at the next available market price, which could be much lower.

If you buy a protective put, you have complete control over when you exercise your option, and the price you're going to receive for your stock is predetermined. However, these benefits do come at a cost. Whereas a stop order is free, you'll have to pay to buy a put. So it would be nice if the stock goes up at least enough to cover the premium paid for the put.

If you buy stock and a protective put at the same time, this is commonly referred to as a "married put." For added enjoyment, feel free to play a wedding march and throw rice while making this trade.

OPTIONS GUY'S TIP:

☞ Many investors will buy a protective put when they've seen a nice run-up on the stock price, and they want to protect their unrealized profits against a downturn. It's sometimes easier to part with the money to pay for the put when you've already seen decent gains on the stock.

BREAK-EVEN AT EXPIRATION

From the point the protective put is established, the break-even point is the current stock price plus the premium paid for the put.

THE SWEET SPOT

You want the stock to go to infinity and the put to expire worthless.

MAXIMUM POTENTIAL PROFIT

Potential profit is theoretically unlimited, because you'll still own the stock and you have not capped the upside.

MAXIMUM POTENTIAL LOSS

Risk is limited to the "deductible" (current stock price minus the strike price) plus the premium paid for the put.

MARGIN REQUIREMENT

After the trade is paid for, no additional margin is required.

AS TIME GOES BY

For this play, time decay is the enemy. It will negatively affect the value of the option you bought.

IMPLIED VOLATILITY

After the play is established, you want implied volatility to increase. That will increase the price of the option you bought.

CHECK YOUR PLAY WITH TRADEKING TOOLS

• Use the *Profit + Loss Calculator* to establish break-even points, evaluate how your strategy might change as expiration approaches, and analyze the Greeks.

COLLAR

THE SETUP

• You own the stock

• Buy a put, strike price A

• Sell a call, strike price B

• Generally, the stock price will be between strikes A and B

NOTE: Both options have the same expiration month.

WHO SHOULD RUN IT

Rookies and higher

WHEN TO RUN IT

  You're bullish but nervous.

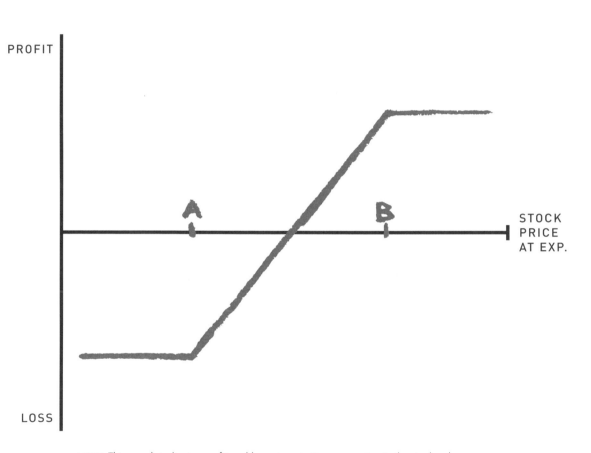

NOTE: This graph indicates profit and loss at expiration, respective to the stock value when you sold the call and bought the put.

THE STRATEGY

Buying the put gives you the right to sell the stock at strike price A. Because you've also sold the call, you'll be obligated to sell the stock at strike price B if the option is assigned.

You can think of a collar as simultaneously running a protective put (play seven) and a covered call (play six). Some investors think this is a sexy trade because the covered call helps to pay for the protective put. So you've limited the downside on the stock for less than it would cost to buy a put alone, but there's a tradeoff.

The call you sell caps the upside. If the stock has exceeded strike B by expiration, it will most likely be called away. So you must be willing to sell it at that price.

OPTIONS GUY'S TIPS:

☞ Many investors will run a collar when they've seen a nice run-up on the stock price, and they want to protect their unrealized profits against a downturn.

☞ Some investors will try to sell the call with enough premium to pay for the put entirely. If established for net-zero cost, it is often referred to as a "zero-cost collar." It may even be established for a net credit, if the call with strike price B is worth more than the put with strike price A.

☞ Some investors will establish this play in a single trade. For every 100 shares they buy, they'll sell one out-of-the-money call contract and buy one out-of-the-money put contract. This limits your downside risk instantly, but of course, it also limits your upside.

⊙ BREAK-EVEN AT EXPIRATION

From the point the collar is established, there are two break-even points:

• If established for a net credit, the break-even is current stock price minus net credit received.

• If established for a net debit, the break-even is current stock price plus the net debit paid.

$ THE SWEET SPOT

You want the stock price to be above strike B at expiration and have the stock called away.

⬆ MAXIMUM POTENTIAL PROFIT

From the point the collar is established, potential profit is limited to strike B minus current stock price minus the net debit paid, or plus net credit received.

⬇ MAXIMUM POTENTIAL LOSS

From the point the collar is established, risk is limited to the current stock price minus strike A plus the net debit paid, or minus the net credit received.

% MARGIN REQUIREMENT

Because you own the stock, the call you sold is considered "covered." So no additional margin is required after the trade is established.

✸ AS TIME GOES BY

For this play, the net effect of time decay is somewhat neutral. It will erode the value of the option you bought (bad) but it will also erode the value of the option you sold (good).

⊕ IMPLIED VOLATILITY

After the play is established, the net effect of an increase in implied volatility is somewhat neutral. The option you sold will increase in value (bad), but it will also increase the value of the option you bought (good).

✔ CHECK YOUR PLAY WITH TRADEKING TOOLS

• Use the *Profit + Loss Calculator* to establish break-even points, evaluate how your strategy might change as expiration approaches, and analyze the Greeks.

FIG LEAF

AKA Leveraged Covered Call; LEAPS
Diagonal Spread

THE SETUP

- Buy an in-the-money LEAPS call, strike price A

- Sell an out-of-the-money short-term call, strike price B

- Generally, the stock price will be closer to strike B than strike A

NOTE: Typically, the LEAPS call will be one to two years from expiration, and the short-term call will be 30 to 45 days from expiration.

WHO SHOULD RUN IT

Veterans and higher

WHEN TO RUN IT

 You're mildly bullish.

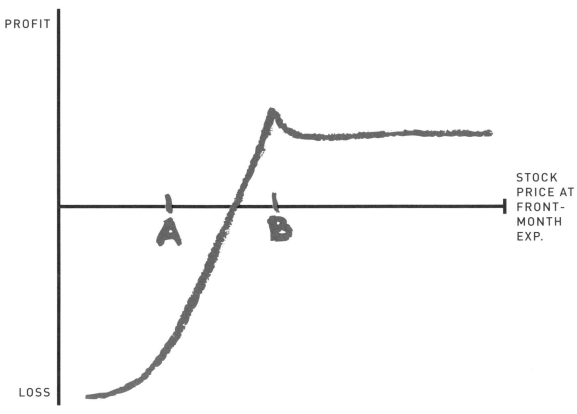

NOTE: The profit and loss lines are not straight. That's because the LEAPS call is still open when the shorter-term call expires. Straight lines and hard angles usually indicate that all options in the play have the same expiration date.

THE STRATEGY

Buying the LEAPS call gives you the right to buy the stock at strike A. Selling the call at strike B obligates you to sell the stock at that strike price if you're assigned.

This play acts like a covered call (play six) but uses the LEAPS call as a surrogate for owning the stock. Though the two plays are similar, managing options with two different expiration dates makes a leveraged covered call a little trickier to run than a regular covered call.

The goal here is to purchase a LEAPS call that will see price changes similar to the stock. So look for a call with a delta of .80 or more. As a starting point, when searching for an appropriate delta, check options that are at least 20% in-the-money. But for a particularly volatile stock, you may need to go deeper in-the-money to find the delta you're looking for.

Some investors favor this strategy over a covered call because you don't have to put up all the capital to buy the stock. That means the premium you receive for selling the call will represent a higher percentage of your initial investment than if you bought the stock outright. In other words, the potential return is leveraged.

Of course, there are additional risks to keep in mind as well: LEAPS, unlike stock, eventually expire. And when they do, it's possible that you could lose the entire value of your initial investment.

Unlike a covered call (where you typically wouldn't mind being assigned on the short option), when running a fig leaf you don't want to be assigned on the short call because you don't actually own the stock yet. You only own the right to buy the stock at strike A.

You wouldn't want to exercise the long LEAPS call to buy the stock because of all the time value you'd give up. Instead, you hope your short call will expire out-of-the-money so you can sell another, and then another, and then another until the long LEAPS call expires.

NOTE: If you are going to run this play, I'm going to make it mandatory for you to read the sections "How We Roll" on P.134 and "What Is Early Exercise and Why Does It Happen?" on P.140.

OPTIONS GUY'S TIPS:

☞ Some investors choose to run this play on an expensive stock that they would like to trade, but don't want to spend the capital to buy at least 100 shares.

☞ If the stock price exceeds the strike price of the short option before expiration, you might want to consider closing out the entire position. If the strategy was implemented correctly, you should see a profit in such a case.

☞ If you do get assigned on the short call, don't make the mistake of exercising the LEAPS call. Sell the LEAPS call on the open market so you'll capture the time value (if there's any remaining) along with the intrinsic value. Simultaneously buy the stock to cover your newly created short stock position. This is a situation when it pays to have a broker who really understands options. So give us a call at TradeKing and we'll help you through the process.

BREAK-EVEN AT EXPIRATION

It is possible to approximate break-even points, but there are too many variables to give an exact formula.

Because there are two expiration dates for the options in a fig leaf, a pricing model must be used to "guesstimate" what the value of the back-month call will be when the front-month call expires. TradeKing's **Profit + Loss Calculator** can help you in this regard. But keep in mind, the **Profit + Loss Calculator** assumes that all other variables, such as implied volatility, interest rates, etc., remain constant over the life of the trade – and they may not behave that way in reality.

THE SWEET SPOT

You want the stock to remain as close to the strike price of the short option as possible at expiration, without going above it.

MAXIMUM POTENTIAL PROFIT

Potential profit is limited to the premium received for sale of the front-month call plus the performance of the LEAPS call.

NOTE: You can't precisely calculate potential profit at initiation of this play, because it depends on how the LEAPS call performs and the premium received for the sale of additional short-term calls (if any) at later dates.

CONTINUED **ON NEXT PAGE**

CONTINUED FROM **FIG LEAF**

⬇ MAXIMUM POTENTIAL LOSS

Potential risk is limited to the debit paid to establish the play.

NOTE: You can't precisely calculate your risk at initiation of this play, because it depends on how the LEAPS call performs and the premium received for the sale of additional short-term calls (if any) at later dates.

% MARGIN REQUIREMENT

After the trade is paid for, no additional margin is required.

⏱ AS TIME GOES BY

Time decay is your friend, because the front-month option(s) you sell will lose their value faster than the back-month long LEAPS call.

⊕ IMPLIED VOLATILITY

After the play is established, the effect of implied volatility is somewhat neutral. Although it will increase the value of the call you sold (bad) it will also increase the value of the LEAPS call you bought (good).

✓ CHECK YOUR PLAY WITH TRADEKING TOOLS

• Use TradeKing's **Profit + Loss Calculator** to establish break-even points, evaluate how your strategy might change as expiration approaches, and analyze the Greeks.

• Use the **Probability Calculator** to determine the probability that the short call will expire out-of-the-money.

Of course, there are risks to keep in mind as well: LEAPS, unlike stock, eventually expire – and when they do, it's possible that you could lose the entire value of your initial investment.

ABOUT THE NAME...

Although this play has been run for quite some time, we at TradeKing have never heard an "official" name for it before. So we decided to give it one.

Special thanks to **Weird Uncle Jesse** from the TradeKing Trader Network for suggesting "fig leaf" (implying you're kind of covered).

Props also go to **TheMechanic** and **MLTrader** for simultaneously suggesting "leveraged covered call" (which is a technically appropriate title).

LONG CALL SPREAD

AKA Bull Call Spread; Vertical Spread

THE SETUP

- Buy a call, strike price A

- Sell a call, strike price B

- Generally, the stock will be at or above strike A and below strike B

NOTE: Both options have the same expiration month.

WHO SHOULD RUN IT

Veterans and higher

WHEN TO RUN IT

 You're bullish, but you have an upside target.

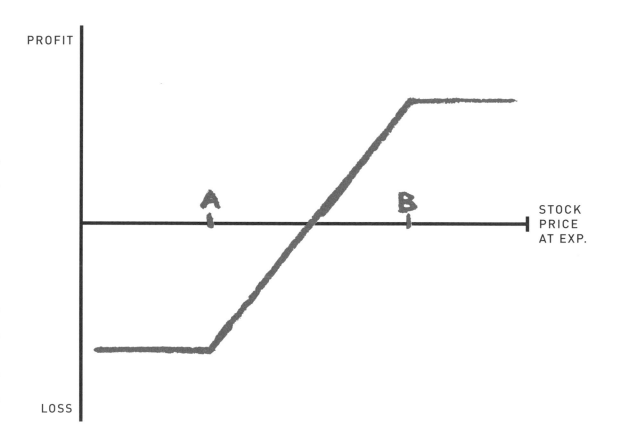

THE STRATEGY

A long call spread gives you the right to buy stock at strike price A and obligates you to sell the stock at strike price B if assigned.

This play is an alternative to buying a long call (play one). Selling a cheaper call with higher-strike B helps to offset the cost of the call you buy at strike A. That ultimately limits your risk. The bad news is, to get the reduction in risk, you're going to have to sacrifice some potential profit.

👤 OPTIONS GUY'S TIPS:

☞ Because you're both buying and selling a call, the potential effect of a decrease in implied volatility will be somewhat neutralized.

☞ The maximum value of a long call spread is usually achieved when it's close to expiration. If you choose to close your position prior to expiration, you'll want as little time value as possible remaining on the call you sold. You may wish to consider buying a shorter-term long call spread, e.g. 30–45 days from expiration.

🔟 BREAK-EVEN AT EXPIRATION

Strike A plus net debit paid.

💲 THE SWEET SPOT

You want the stock to be at or above strike B at expiration, but not so far that you're disappointed you didn't simply buy a call on the underlying stock. But look on the bright side if that does happen – you played it smart and made a profit, and that's always a good thing.

⬆ MAXIMUM POTENTIAL PROFIT

Potential profit is limited to the difference between strike A and strike B minus the net debit paid.

⬇ MAXIMUM POTENTIAL LOSS

Risk is limited to the net debit paid.

% MARGIN REQUIREMENT

After the trade is paid for, no additional margin is required.

☯ AS TIME GOES BY

For this play, the net effect of time decay is somewhat neutral. It's eroding the value of the option you purchased (bad) and the option you sold (good).

⊕ IMPLIED VOLATILITY

After the play is established, the effect of implied volatility depends on where the stock is relative to your strike prices.

If your forecast was correct and the stock price is approaching or above strike B, you want implied volatility to decrease. That's because it will decrease the value of the near-the-money option you sold faster than the in-the-money option you bought, thereby increasing the overall value of the spread.

If your forecast was incorrect and the stock price is approaching or below strike A, you want implied volatility to increase for two reasons. First, it will increase the value of the option you bought faster than the out-of-the-money option you sold, thereby increasing the overall value of the spread. Second, it reflects an increased probability of a price swing (which will hopefully be to the upside).

✔ CHECK YOUR PLAY WITH TRADEKING TOOLS

• Use the *Profit + Loss Calculator* to establish break-even points, evaluate how your strategy might change as expiration approaches, and analyze the Greeks.

• Use the *Technical Analysis Tool* to look for bullish indicators.

LONG PUT SPREAD

AKA Bear Put Spread; Vertical Spread

THE SETUP

- Sell a put, strike price A
- Buy a put, strike price B
- Generally, the stock will be at or below strike B and above strike A

NOTE: Both options have the same expiration month.

WHO SHOULD RUN IT

Veterans and higher

WHEN TO RUN IT

 You're bearish, with a downside target.

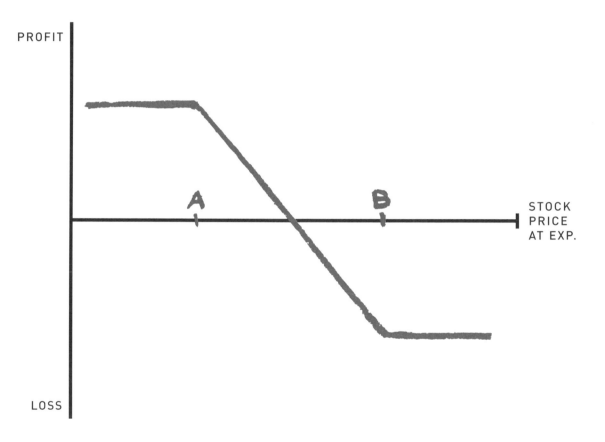

THE STRATEGY

A long put spread gives you the right to sell stock at strike price B and obligates you to buy stock at strike price A if assigned.

This play is an alternative to buying a long put (play two). Selling a cheaper put with strike A helps to offset the cost of the put you buy with strike B. That ultimately limits your risk. The bad news is, to get the reduction in risk, you're going to have to sacrifice some potential profit.

👤 OPTIONS GUY'S TIPS:

☞ When implied volatility is unusually high (e.g., around earnings) consider a long put spread as an alternative to merely buying a put alone. Because you're both buying and selling a put, the potential effect of a decrease in implied volatility will be somewhat neutralized.

☞ The maximum value of a long put spread is usually achieved when it's close to expiration. If you choose to close your position prior to expiration, you'll want as little time value as possible remaining on the put you sold. You may wish to consider buying a shorter-term long put spread, e.g., 30–45 days from expiration.

🔟 BREAK-EVEN AT EXPIRATION

Strike B minus the net debit paid.

💲 THE SWEET SPOT

You want the stock to be at or below strike A at expiration.

⬆ MAXIMUM POTENTIAL PROFIT

Potential profit is limited to the difference between strike A and strike B, minus the net debit paid.

⬇ MAXIMUM POTENTIAL LOSS

Risk is limited to the net debit paid.

% MARGIN REQUIREMENT

After the trade is paid for, no additional margin is required.

⏱ AS TIME GOES BY

For this play, the net effect of time decay is somewhat neutral. It's eroding the value of the option you bought (bad) and the option you sold (good).

◑ IMPLIED VOLATILITY

After the play is established, the effect of implied volatility depends on where the stock is relative to your strike prices.

If your forecast was correct and the stock price is approaching or below strike A, you want implied volatility to decrease. That's because it will decrease the value of the near-the-money option you sold faster than the in-the-money option you bought, thereby increasing the overall value of the spread.

If your forecast was incorrect and the stock price is approaching or above strike B, you want implied volatility to increase for two reasons. First, it will increase the value of the out-of-the-money option you bought faster than the near-the-money option you sold, thereby increasing the overall value of the spread. Second, it reflects an increased probability of a price swing (which will hopefully be to the downside).

✓ CHECK YOUR PLAY WITH TRADEKING TOOLS

• Use the **Profit + Loss Calculator** to establish break-even points, evaluate how your strategy might change as expiration approaches, and analyze the Greeks.

• Use the **Technical Analysis Tool** to look for bearish indicators.

SHORT CALL SPREAD

AKA Bear Call Spread; Vertical Spread

THE SETUP

- Sell a call, strike price A
- Buy a call, strike price B
- Generally, the stock will be below strike A

NOTE: Both options have the same expiration month.

WHO SHOULD RUN IT

Seasoned Veterans and higher

WHEN TO RUN IT

  You're bearish. You may also be expecting neutral activity if strike A is out-of-the-money.

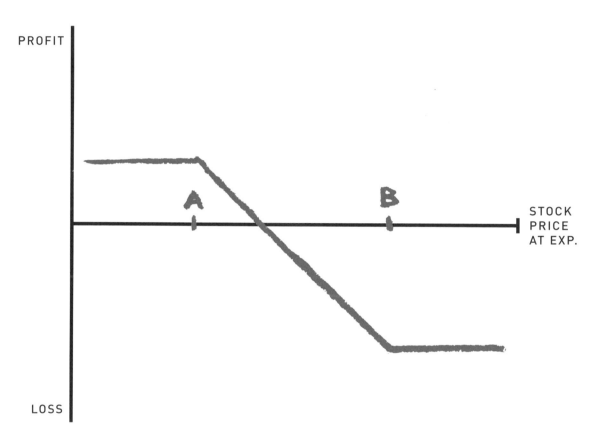

THE STRATEGY

A short call spread obligates you to sell the stock at strike price A if the option is assigned but gives you the right to buy stock at strike price B.

A short call spread is an alternative to the short call (play three). In addition to selling a call with strike A, you're buying the cheaper call with strike B to limit your risk if the stock goes up. But there's a tradeoff – buying the call also reduces the net credit received when running the play.

🧑 OPTIONS GUY'S TIPS:

☞ One advantage of this play is that you want both options to expire worthless. If that happens, you won't have to pay any commissions to get out of your position.

☞ You may wish to consider ensuring that strike A is around one standard deviation out-of-the-money at initiation. That will increase your probability of success. However, the further out-of-the-money the strike price is, the lower the net credit received will be from this play.

☞ As a general rule of thumb, you may wish to consider running this play approximately 30–45 days from expiration to take advantage of accelerating time decay as expiration approaches. Of course, this depends on the underlying stock and market conditions such as implied volatility.

⓪ BREAK-EVEN AT EXPIRATION

Strike A plus the net credit received when opening the position.

⑤ THE SWEET SPOT

You want the stock price to be at or below strike A at expiration, so both options expire worthless.

⬆ MAXIMUM POTENTIAL PROFIT

Potential profit is limited to the net credit received when opening the position.

⬇ MAXIMUM POTENTIAL LOSS

Risk is limited to the difference between strike A and strike B, minus the net credit received.

% MARGIN REQUIREMENT

See Appendix A for margin requirement.

⏱ AS TIME GOES BY

For this play, the net effect of time decay is somewhat positive. It will erode the value of the option you sold (good) but it will also erode the value of the option you bought (bad).

⊕ IMPLIED VOLATILITY

After the play is established, the effect of implied volatility depends on where the stock is relative to your strike prices.

If your forecast was correct and the stock price is approaching or below strike A, you want implied volatility to decrease. That's because it will decrease the value of both options, and ideally you want them to expire worthless.

If your forecast was incorrect and the stock price is approaching or above strike B, you want implied volatility to increase for two reasons. First, it will increase the value of the near-the-money option you bought faster than the in-the-money option you sold, thereby decreasing the overall value of the spread. Second, it reflects an increased probability of a price swing (which will hopefully be to the downside).

✔ CHECK YOUR PLAY WITH TRADEKING TOOLS

• Use the **Profit + Loss Calculator** to establish break-even points and evaluate how your strategy might change as expiration approaches, depending on the Greeks.

• Use the **Technical Analysis Tool** to look for bearish indicators.

• Use the **Probability Calculator** to verify that strike A is about one standard deviation out-of-the-money.

SHORT PUT SPREAD

AKA Bull Put Spread; Vertical Spread

THE SETUP

- Buy a put, strike price A
- Sell a put, strike price B
- Generally, the stock will be above strike B

NOTE: Both options have the same expiration month.

WHO SHOULD RUN IT

Seasoned Veterans and higher

WHEN TO RUN IT

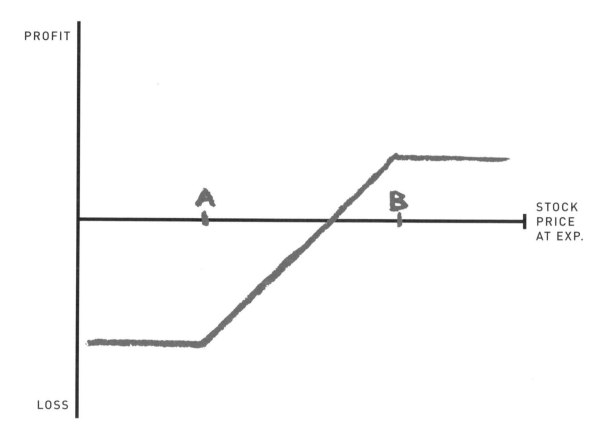

You're bullish. You may also be anticipating neutral activity if strike B is out-of-the-money.

THE STRATEGY

A short put spread obligates you to buy the stock at strike price B if the option is assigned but gives you the right to sell stock at strike price A.

A short put spread is an alternative to the short put (play four). In addition to selling a put with strike B, you're buying the cheaper put with strike A to limit your risk if the stock goes down. But there's a tradeoff – buying the put also reduces the net credit received when running the play.

👤 OPTIONS GUY'S TIPS:

☞ One advantage of this play is that you want both options to expire worthless. If that happens, you won't have to pay any commissions to get out of your position.

☞ You may wish to consider ensuring that strike B is around one standard deviation out-of-the-money at initiation. That will increase your probability of success. However, the further out-of-the-money the strike price is, the lower the net credit received will be from this spread.

☞ As a general rule of thumb, you may wish to consider running this play approximately 30–45 days from expiration to take advantage of accelerating time decay as expiration approaches. Of course, this depends on the underlying stock and market conditions such as implied volatility.

⓪ BREAK-EVEN AT EXPIRATION

Strike B minus the net credit received when selling the spread.

$ THE SWEET SPOT

You want the stock to be at or above strike B at expiration, so both options will expire worthless.

⬆ MAXIMUM POTENTIAL PROFIT

Potential profit is limited to the net credit you receive when you set up the play.

⬇ MAXIMUM POTENTIAL LOSS

Risk is limited to the difference between strike A and strike B, minus the net credit received.

% MARGIN REQUIREMENT

See Appendix A for margin requirement.

⏱ AS TIME GOES BY

For this play, the net effect of time decay is somewhat positive. It will erode the value of the option you sold (good) but it will also erode the value of the option you bought (bad).

📈 IMPLIED VOLATILITY

After the play is established, the effect of implied volatility depends on where the stock is relative to your strike prices.

If your forecast was correct and the stock price is approaching or above strike B, you want implied volatility to decrease. That's because it will decrease the value of both options, and ideally you want them to expire worthless.

If your forecast was incorrect and the stock price is approaching or below strike A, you want implied volatility to increase for two reasons. First, it will increase the value of the near-the-money option you bought faster than the in-the-money option you sold, thereby decreasing the overall value of the spread. Second, it reflects an increased probability of a price swing (which will hopefully be to the upside).

✅ CHECK YOUR PLAY WITH TRADEKING TOOLS

• Use the *Profit + Loss Calculator* to establish break-even points and evaluate how your strategy might change as expiration approaches, depending on the Greeks.

• Use the *Technical Analysis Tool* to look for bullish indicators.

• Use the *Probability Calculator* to verify that strike B is about one standard deviation out-of-the-money.

LONG STRADDLE

THE SETUP

- Buy a call, strike price A
- Buy a put, strike price A
- Generally, the stock price will be at strike A

NOTE: Both options have the same expiration month.

WHO SHOULD RUN IT

Seasoned Veterans and higher

NOTE: At first glance, this seems like a fairly simple play. However, it is not suited for all investors. To profit from a long straddle, you'll require fairly advanced forecasting ability.

WHEN TO RUN IT

You're anticipating a swing in stock price, but you're not sure which direction it will go.

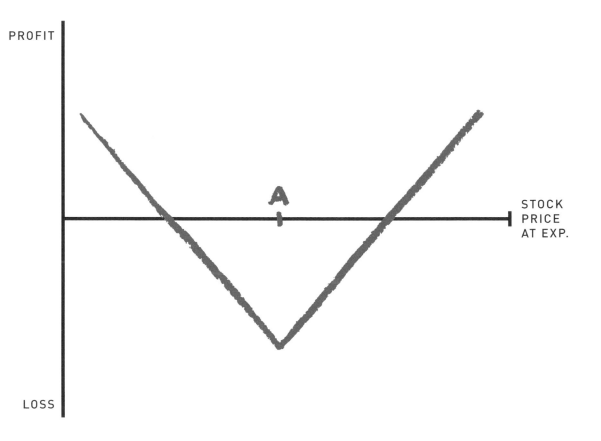

THE STRATEGY

A long straddle is the best of both worlds, since the call gives you the right to buy the stock at strike price A and the put gives you the right to sell the stock at strike price A. But those rights don't come cheap.

The goal is to profit if the stock moves in either direction. Typically, a straddle will be constructed with the call and put at-the-money (or at the nearest strike price if there's not one exactly at-the-money). Buying both a call and a put increases the cost of your position, especially for a volatile stock. So you'll need a fairly significant price swing just to break even.

Advanced traders might run this play to take advantage of a possible increase in implied volatility. If implied volatility is abnormally low for no apparent reason, the call and put may be undervalued. The idea is to buy them at a discount, then wait for implied volatility to rise and close the position at a profit.

👤 OPTIONS GUY'S TIPS:

☞ Many investors who use the long straddle will look for major news events that may cause the stock to make an abnormally large move. For example, they'll consider running this play prior to an earnings announcement that might send the stock in either direction.

☞ If buying a short-term straddle (perhaps two weeks or less) prior to an earnings announcement, look at the stock's charts on TradeKing.com. There's a checkbox that allows you to see the dates when earnings were announced. Look for instances where the stock moved at least 1.5 times more than the cost of your straddle. If the stock didn't move at least that much on any of the last three earnings announcements, you probably shouldn't run this play. Lie down until the urge goes away.

⑪ BREAK-EVEN POINTS AT EXPIRATION

There are two break-even points:

- Strike A plus the net debit paid.
- Strike A minus the net debit paid.

💲 THE SWEET SPOT

The stock shoots to the moon, or goes straight down the toilet.

⬆ MAXIMUM POTENTIAL PROFIT

Potential profit is theoretically unlimited if the stock goes up.

If the stock goes down, potential profit may be substantial but limited to the strike price minus the net debit paid.

⬇ MAXIMUM POTENTIAL LOSS

Potential losses are limited to the net debit paid.

％ MARGIN REQUIREMENT

After the trade is paid for, no additional margin is required.

🕐 AS TIME GOES BY

For this play, time decay is your mortal enemy. It will cause the value of both options to decrease, so it's working doubly against you.

⚡ IMPLIED VOLATILITY

After the play is established, you really want implied volatility to increase. It will increase the value of both options, and it also suggests an increased possibility of a price swing. Huzzah.

Conversely, a decrease in implied volatility will be doubly painful because it will work against both options you bought. If you run this play, you can really get hurt by a volatility crunch.

✅ CHECK YOUR PLAY WITH TRADEKING TOOLS

- Use the **Profit + Loss Calculator** to establish break-even points, evaluate how your strategy might change as expiration approaches, and analyze the Greeks.

- Examine the stock's **Volatility Charts**. If you're doing this as a volatility play, you want to see implied volatility abnormally low compared to historic volatility.

SHORT STRADDLE

THE SETUP

• Sell a call, strike price A

• Sell a put, strike price A

• Generally, the stock price will be at strike A

NOTE: Both options have the same expiration month.

WHO SHOULD RUN IT

All-Stars only

NOTE: This play is only suited for the most advanced traders and not for the faint of heart. Short straddles are mainly for market professionals who watch their account full-time. In other words, this is not a trade you manage from the golf course.

WHEN TO RUN IT

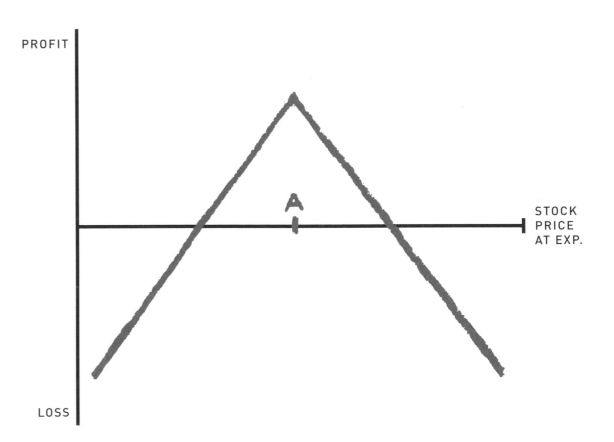

(N) You're expecting minimal movement on the stock. (In fact, you should be darn certain that the stock will stick close to strike A.)

THE STRATEGY

A short straddle gives you the obligation to sell the stock at strike price A and the obligation to buy the stock at strike price A if the options are assigned.

By selling two options, you significantly increase the income you would have achieved from selling a put or a call alone. But that comes at a cost. You have unlimited risk on the upside and substantial downside risk.

Advanced traders might run this play to take advantage of a possible decrease in implied volatility. If implied volatility is abnormally high for no apparent reason, the call and put may be overvalued. After the sale, the idea is to wait for volatility to drop and close the position at a profit.

👤 OPTIONS GUY'S TIP:

☞ Even if you're willing to accept high risk, you may wish to consider a short strangle (play seventeen) since its sweet spot is wider than a short straddle's.

🔟 BREAK-EVEN AT EXPIRATION

There are two break-even points:

- Strike A minus the net credit received.
- Strike A plus the net credit received.

💲 THE SWEET SPOT

You want the stock exactly at strike A at expiration, so the options expire worthless. However, that's extremely difficult to predict. Good luck with that.

⬆ MAXIMUM POTENTIAL PROFIT

Potential profit is limited to the net credit received for selling the call and the put.

⬇ MAXIMUM POTENTIAL LOSS

If the stock goes up, your losses could be theoretically unlimited.

If the stock goes down, your losses may be substantial but limited to the strike price minus net credit received for selling the straddle.

% MARGIN REQUIREMENT

See Appendix A for margin requirement.

🕑 AS TIME GOES BY

For this play, time decay is your best friend. It works doubly in your favor, eroding the price of both options you sold. That means if you choose to close your position prior to expiration, it will be less expensive to buy it back.

⊕ IMPLIED VOLATILITY

After the play is established, you really want implied volatility to decrease. An increase in implied volatility is dangerous because it works doubly against you by increasing the price of both options you sold. That means if you wish to close your position prior to expiration, it will be more expensive to buy back those options.

An increase in implied volatility also suggests an increased possibility of a price swing, whereas you want the stock price to remain stable around strike A.

✔ CHECK YOUR PLAY WITH TRADEKING TOOLS

- Use the *Profit + Loss Calculator* to establish break-even points, evaluate how your strategy might change as expiration approaches, and analyze the Greeks.

- Examine the stock's *Volatility Charts*. If you're doing this as a volatility play, you want to see implied volatility abnormally high compared with historic volatility.

LONG STRANGLE

THE SETUP

- Buy a put, strike price A

- Buy a call, strike price B

- Generally, the stock price will be between strikes A and B

NOTE: Both options have the same expiration month.

WHO SHOULD RUN IT

Seasoned Veterans and higher

NOTE: Like the long straddle, this seems like a fairly simple play. However, it is not suited for all investors. To profit from a long strangle, you'll require fairly advanced forecasting ability.

WHEN TO RUN IT

(?) You're anticipating a swing in stock price, but you're not sure which direction it will go.

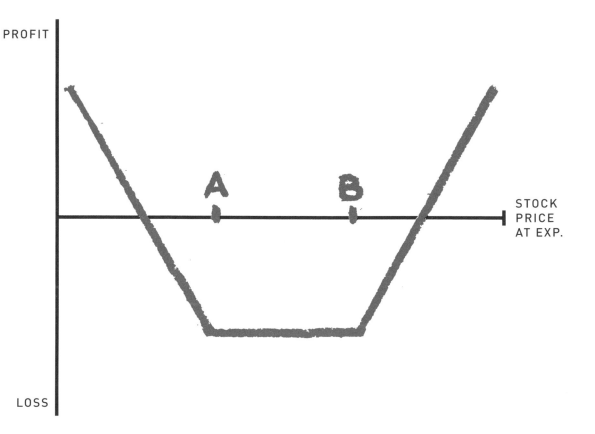

PROFIT

LOSS

STOCK PRICE AT EXP.

A B

THE STRATEGY

A long strangle gives you the right to sell the stock at strike price A and the right to buy the stock at strike price B.

The goal is to profit if the stock makes a move in either direction. However, buying both a call and a put increases the cost of your position, especially for a volatile stock. So you'll need a significant price swing just to break even.

The difference between a long strangle and a long straddle (play fourteen) is that you separate the strike prices for the two legs of the trade. That reduces the net cost of running this play, since the options you buy will be out-of-the-money. The tradeoff is, because you're dealing with an out-of-the-money call and an out-of-the-money put, the stock will need to move even more significantly before you make a profit.

👤 OPTIONS GUY'S TIPS:

☞ Many investors who use the long strangle will look for major news events that may cause the stock to make an abnormally large move. For example, they'll consider running this play prior to an earnings announcement that might send the stock in either direction.

☞ Unless you're dead certain the stock is going to make a very large move, you may wish to consider running a long straddle instead of a long strangle. Although a straddle costs more to run, the stock won't have to make such a large move to reach your break-even points.

🕙 BREAK-EVEN AT EXPIRATION

There are two break-even points:

- Strike A minus the net debit paid.

- Strike B plus the net debit paid.

💲 THE SWEET SPOT

The stock shoots to the moon, or goes straight down the toilet.

⬆ MAXIMUM POTENTIAL PROFIT

Potential profit is theoretically unlimited if the stock goes up.

If the stock goes down, potential profit may be substantial but limited to strike A minus the net debit paid.

⬇ MAXIMUM POTENTIAL LOSS

Potential losses are limited to the net debit paid.

% MARGIN REQUIREMENT

After the trade is paid for, no additional margin is required.

🕗 AS TIME GOES BY

For this play, time decay is your mortal enemy. It will cause the value of both options to decrease, so it's working doubly against you.

✴ IMPLIED VOLATILITY

After the play is established, you really want implied volatility to increase. It will increase the value of both options, and it also suggests an increased possibility of a price swing. Sweet.

Conversely, a decrease in implied volatility will be doubly painful because it will work against both options you bought. If you run this play, you can really get hurt by a volatility crunch.

✔ CHECK YOUR PLAY WITH TRADEKING TOOLS

- Use the *Profit + Loss Calculator* to establish break-even points, evaluate how your strategy might change as expiration approaches, and analyze the Greeks.

SHORT STRANGLE

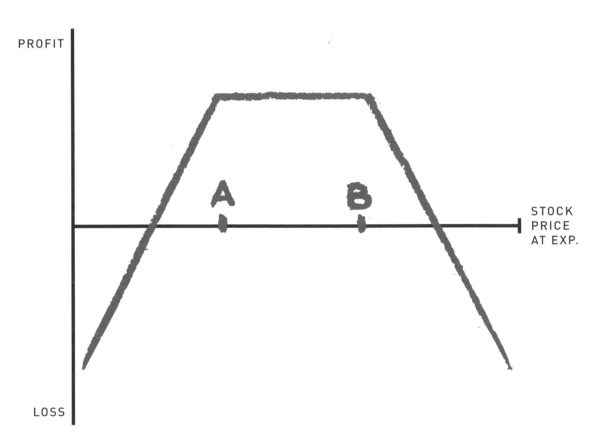

PROFIT

A   B

STOCK
PRICE
AT EXP.

LOSS

THE SETUP

• Sell a put, strike price A

• Sell a call, strike price B

• Generally, the stock price will be between strikes A and B

NOTE: Both options have the same expiration month.

WHO SHOULD RUN IT

All-Stars only

NOTE: This play is only for the most advanced traders who like to live dangerously (and watch their accounts constantly).

WHEN TO RUN IT

 You are anticipating minimal movement on the stock.

THE STRATEGY

A short strangle gives you the obligation to buy the stock at strike price A and the obligation to sell the stock at strike price B if the options are assigned. You are predicting the stock price will remain somewhere between strike A and strike B, and the options you sell will expire worthless.

By selling two options, you significantly increase the income you would have achieved from selling a put or a call alone. But that comes at a cost. You have unlimited risk on the upside and substantial downside risk. To avoid being exposed to such risk, you may wish to consider using an iron condor instead (play thirty-nine).

Like the short straddle (play fifteen), advanced traders might run this play to take advantage of a possible decrease in implied volatility. If implied volatility is abnormally high for no apparent reason, the call and put may be overvalued. After the sale, the idea is to wait for volatility to drop and close the position at a profit.

👤 OPTIONS GUY'S TIP:

☞ You may wish to consider ensuring that strike A and strike B are one standard deviation or more away from the stock price at initiation. That will increase your probability of success. However, the further out-of-the-money the strike prices are, the lower the net credit received will be from this play.

⓪ BREAK-EVEN AT EXPIRATION

There are two break-even points:

- Strike A minus the net credit received.
- Strike B plus the net credit received.

💲 THE SWEET SPOT

You want the stock at or between strikes A and B at expiration, so the options expire worthless.

⬆ MAXIMUM POTENTIAL PROFIT

Potential profit is limited to the net credit received.

⬇ MAXIMUM POTENTIAL LOSS

If the stock goes up, your losses could be theoretically unlimited.

If the stock goes down, your losses may be substantial but limited to strike A minus the net credit received.

% MARGIN REQUIREMENT

See Appendix A for margin requirement.

🕑 AS TIME GOES BY

For this play, time decay is your best friend. It works doubly in your favor, eroding the price of both options you sold. That means if you choose to close your position prior to expiration, it will be less expensive to buy it back.

⟡ IMPLIED VOLATILITY

After the play is established, you really want implied volatility to decrease. An increase in implied volatility is dangerous because it works doubly against you by increasing the price of both options you sold. That means if you wish to close your position prior to expiration, it will be more expensive to buy back those options.

An increase in implied volatility also suggests an increased possibility of a price swing, whereas you want the stock price to remain stable between strike A and strike B.

✔ CHECK YOUR PLAY WITH TRADEKING TOOLS

- Use the *Profit + Loss Calculator* to establish break-even points, evaluate how your strategy might change as expiration approaches, and analyze the Greeks.

- Use the *Probability Calculator* to verify that both the call and put you sell are about one standard deviation out-of-the-money.

- Examine the stock's *Volatility Charts*. If you're doing this as a volatility play, you want to see implied volatility abnormally high compared with historic volatility.

LONG COMBINATION

AKA Synthetic Long Stock; Combo

THE SETUP

- Buy a call, strike price A
- Sell a put, strike price A
- The stock should be at or very near strike A

WHO SHOULD RUN IT

All-Stars only

NOTE: The short put in this play creates substantial risk. That is why it is only for the most advanced option traders.

WHEN TO RUN IT

 You're bullish.

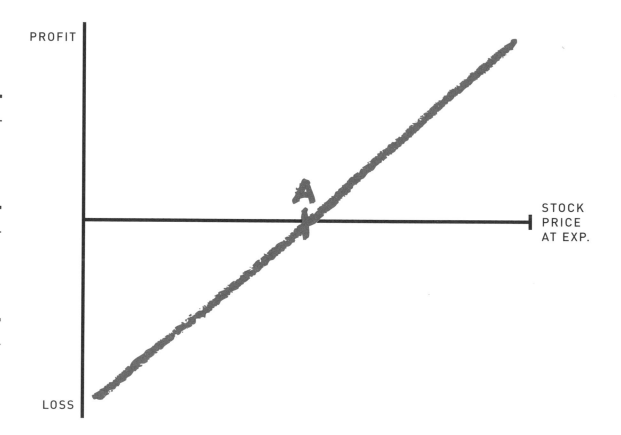

THE STRATEGY

Buying the call gives you the right to buy the stock at strike price A. Selling the put obligates you to buy the stock at strike price A if the option is assigned.

This play is often referred to as "synthetic long stock" because the risk / reward profile is nearly identical to long stock. Furthermore, if you remain in this position until expiration, you will probably wind up buying the stock at strike A one way or the other. If the stock is above strike A at expiration, it would make sense to exercise the call and buy the stock. If the stock is below strike A at expiration, you'll most likely be assigned on the put and be required to buy the stock.

Since you'll have the same risk / reward profile as long stock at expiration, you might be wondering, "Why would I want to run a combination instead of buying the stock?" The answer is leverage. You can achieve the same end without the up-front cost to buy the stock.

At initiation of the play, you will have some additional margin requirements in your account because of the short put, and you can also expect to pay a net debit to establish your position. But those costs will be fairly small relative to the price of the stock.

Most people who run a combination don't intend to remain in the position until expiration, so they won't wind up buying the stock. They're simply doing it for the leverage.

👤 OPTIONS GUY'S TIPS:

☞ It's important to note that the stock price will rarely be precisely at strike price A when you establish this play. If the stock price is above strike A, the long call will usually cost more than the short put. So the play will be established for a net debit. If the stock price is below strike A, you will usually receive more for the short put than you pay for the long call. So the play will be established for a net credit. Remember: The net debit paid or net credit received to establish this play will be affected by where the stock price is relative to the strike price.

☞ Dividends and carry costs can also play a large role in this play. For instance, if a company that has never paid a dividend before suddenly announces it's going to start paying one, it will affect call and put prices almost immediately. That's because the stock price will be expected to drop by the amount of the dividend after the ex-dividend date. As a result, put prices will increase and call prices will decrease independently of stock price movement in anticipation of the dividend. If the cost of puts exceeds the price of calls, then you will be able to establish this play for a net credit. The moral of this story is: Dividends will affect whether or not you will be able to establish this play for a net credit instead of a net debit. So keep an eye out for them if you're considering this play.

🔟 BREAK-EVEN AT EXPIRATION

Strike A plus the net debit paid or minus the net credit received to establish the play.

💲 THE SWEET SPOT

You want the stock to shoot through the roof.

⬆ MAXIMUM POTENTIAL PROFIT

There is a theoretically unlimited profit potential if the stock price keeps rising.

⬇ MAXIMUM POTENTIAL LOSS

Potential loss is substantial, but limited to strike price A plus the net debit paid or minus net credit received.

% MARGIN REQUIREMENT

See Appendix A for margin requirement.

❄ AS TIME GOES BY

For this play, time decay is somewhat neutral. It will erode the value of the option you bought (bad) but it will also erode the value of the option you sold (good).

◑ IMPLIED VOLATILITY

After the play is established, increasing implied volatility is somewhat neutral. It will increase the value of the option you sold (bad) but it will also increase the value of the option you bought (good).

✅ CHECK YOUR PLAY WITH TRADEKING TOOLS

• Use TradeKing's *Profit + Loss Calculator* to establish break-even points, evaluate how your strategy might change as expiration approaches, and analyze the Greeks.

• Use the *Technical Analysis Tool* to look for bullish indicators.

SHORT COMBINATION

AKA Synthetic Short Stock; Combo

THE SETUP

- Sell a call, strike price A

- Buy a put, strike price A

- The stock should be at or very near strike A

WHO SHOULD RUN IT

All-Stars only

NOTE: The short call in this play creates theoretically unlimited risk. That is why it is only for the most advanced option traders.

WHEN TO RUN IT

 You're bearish.

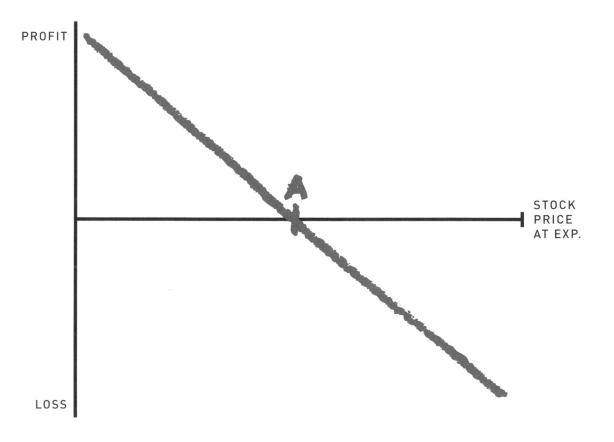

THE STRATEGY

Buying the put gives you the right to sell the stock at strike price A. Selling the call obligates you to sell the stock at strike price A if the option is assigned.

This play is often referred to as "synthetic short stock" because the risk / reward profile is nearly identical to short stock.

If you remain in this position until expiration, you are probably going to wind up selling the stock one way or the other. If the stock price is above strike A, the call will be assigned, resulting in a short sale of the stock. If the stock is below strike A, it would make sense to exercise your put and sell the stock. However, most investors who run this play don't plan to stay in their position until expiration.

At initiation of the play, you will most likely receive a net credit, but you will have some additional margin requirements in your account because of the short call. However, those costs will be fairly small relative to the margin requirement for short stock. That's the reason some investors run this play: to avoid having too much cash tied up in margin created by a short stock position.

👤 OPTIONS GUY'S TIPS:

☞ It's important to note that the stock price will rarely be precisely at strike price A when you establish this play. If the stock price is above strike A, you'll receive more for the short call than you pay for the long put. So the play will be established for a net credit. If the stock price is below strike A, you will usually pay more for the long put than you receive for the short call. So the play will be established for a net debit. Remember:

The net credit received or net debit paid to establish this play will be affected by where the stock price is relative to the strike price.

☞ Dividends and carry costs can also play a large role in this play. For instance, if a company that has never paid a dividend before suddenly announces it's going to start paying one, it will affect call and put prices almost immediately. That's because the stock price will be expected to drop by the amount of the dividend after the ex-dividend date. As a result, put prices will increase and call prices will decrease independently of stock price movement in anticipation of the dividend. If the cost of puts exceeds the price of calls, then you will have to establish this play for a net debit. The moral of this story is: Dividends will affect whether or not you will be able to establish this play for a net credit instead of a net debit. So keep an eye out for them if you're considering this play.

☞ On the other hand, you may want to consider running this play on stock you want to short but that has a pending dividend. If you are short stock, you will be required to pay any dividends out of your own account. But with this play, you'll have no such requirement.

⓪ BREAK-EVEN AT EXPIRATION

Strike A plus the net credit received or minus the net debit paid to establish the play.

$ THE SWEET SPOT

You want the stock to completely tank.

↑ MAXIMUM POTENTIAL PROFIT

Potential profit is substantial if stock goes to zero, but limited to strike price A plus the net credit received or minus the net debit paid to establish the play.

↓ MAXIMUM POTENTIAL LOSS

Risk is theoretically unlimited if the stock price keeps rising.

% MARGIN REQUIREMENT

See Appendix A for margin requirement.

🕐 AS TIME GOES BY

For this play, time decay is somewhat neutral. It will erode the value of the option you bought (bad) but it will also erode the value of the option you sold (good).

✚ IMPLIED VOLATILITY

After the play is established, increasing implied volatility is somewhat neutral. It will increase the value of the option you sold (bad) but it will also increase the value of the option you bought (good).

✓ CHECK YOUR PLAY WITH TRADEKING TOOLS

• Use TradeKing's *Profit + Loss Calculator* to establish break-even points, evaluate how your strategy might change as expiration approaches, and analyze the Greeks.

• Use the *Technical Analysis Tool* to look for bearish indicators.

FRONT SPREAD W/ CALLS

AKA Ratio Vertical Spread

THE SETUP

- Buy a call, strike price A
- Sell two calls, strike price B
- Generally, the stock will be below or at strike A

NOTE: All options have the same expiration month.

WHO SHOULD RUN IT

All-Stars only

NOTE: Due to the unlimited risk if the stock moves significantly higher, this play is suited only to the most advanced option traders. If you are not an All-Star trader, consider running a skip strike butterfly with calls.

WHEN TO RUN IT

 You're slightly bullish. You want the stock to rise to strike B and then stop.

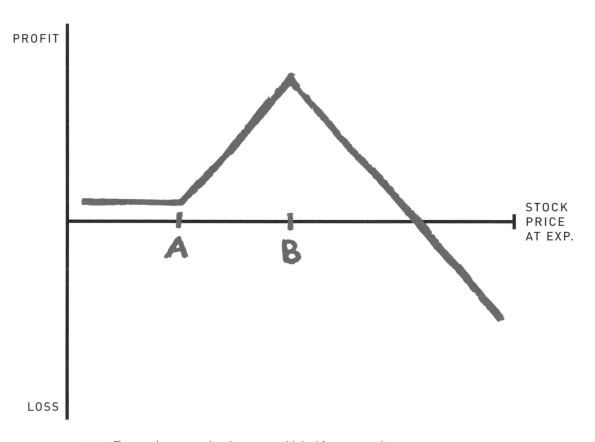

NOTE: This graph assumes the play was established for a net credit.

THE STRATEGY

Buying the call gives you the right to buy stock at strike price A. Selling the two calls gives you the obligation to sell stock at strike price B if the options are assigned.

This play enables you to purchase a call that is at-the-money or slightly out-of-the-money without paying full price. The goal is to obtain the call with strike A for a credit or a very small debit by selling the two calls with strike B.

Ideally, you want a slight rise in stock price to strike B. But watch out. Although one of the calls you sold is "covered" by the call you buy with strike A, the second call you sold is "uncovered," exposing you to theoretically unlimited risk.

If the stock goes too high, you'll be in for a world of hurt. So beware of any abnormal moves in stock price and have a stop-loss plan in place.

👤 OPTIONS GUY'S TIPS:

☞ Some investors may wish to run this play using index options rather than options on individual stocks. That's because historically, indexes have not been as volatile as individual stocks. Fluctuations in an index's component stock prices tend to cancel one another out, lessening the volatility of the index as a whole.

☞ The maximum value of a front spread is usually achieved when it's close to expiration. You may wish to consider running this play shorter-term; e.g., 30–45 days from expiration.

☞ If you're not approved to sell uncovered calls, consider buying the stock at the same time you set up this play. That way, the second call won't be uncovered, and this play will be like a covered call on steroids.

🔟 BREAK-EVEN AT EXPIRATION

If established for a net debit, there are two break-even points:

• Strike A plus net debit paid to establish the position.

• Strike B plus the maximum profit potential.

If established for a net credit, there is only one break-even point:

• Strike B plus the maximum profit potential.

💲 THE SWEET SPOT

You want the stock price exactly at strike B at expiration.

⬆ MAXIMUM POTENTIAL PROFIT

If established for a net debit, potential profit is limited to the difference between strike A and strike B, minus the net debit paid.

If established for a net credit, potential profit is limited to the difference between strike A and strike B, plus the net credit.

⬇ MAXIMUM POTENTIAL LOSS

If established for a net debit:

• Risk is limited to the debit paid for the spread if the stock price goes down.

• Risk is unlimited if the stock price goes way, way up.

If established for a net credit:

• Risk is unlimited if the stock price goes way, way up.

% MARGIN REQUIREMENT

See Appendix A for margin requirement.

🕐 AS TIME GOES BY

For this play, time decay is your friend. It's eroding the value of the option you purchased (bad). However, that will be outweighed by the decrease in value of the two options you sold (good).

🔆 IMPLIED VOLATILITY

After the play is established, in general you want implied volatility to go down. That's because it will decrease the value of the two options you sold more than the single option you bought.

The closer the stock price is to strike B, the more you want implied volatility to decrease for two reasons. First, it will decrease the value of the near-the-money options you sold at strike B more than the in-the-money option you bought at strike A. Second, it suggests a decreased probability of a wide price swing, whereas you want the stock price to remain stable at or around strike B and finish there at expiration.

✓ CHECK YOUR PLAY WITH TRADEKING TOOLS

• Use the *Profit + Loss Calculator* to establish break-even points, evaluate how your strategy might change as expiration approaches, and analyze the Greeks.

FRONT SPREAD W/ PUTS

AKA Ratio Vertical Spread

THE SETUP

- Sell two puts, strike price A

- Buy a put, strike price B

- Generally, the stock will be at or above strike B

NOTE: All options have the same expiration month.

WHO SHOULD RUN IT

All-Stars only

NOTE: Due to the significant risk if the stock moves sharply downward, this play is suited only to the most advanced option traders. If you are not an All-Star trader, consider running a skip strike butterfly with puts.

WHEN TO RUN IT

 You're slightly bearish. You want the stock to go down to strike A and then stop.

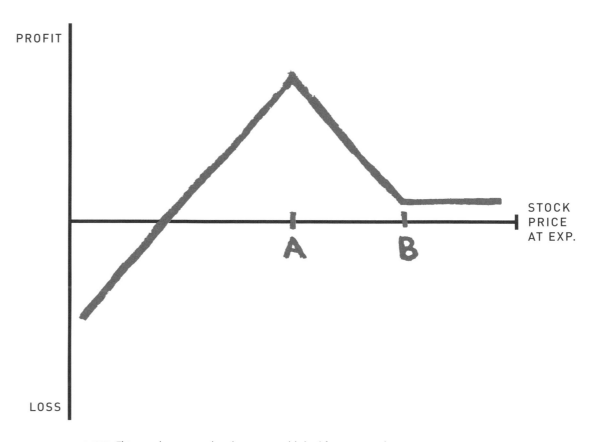

NOTE: This graph assumes the play was established for a net credit.

THE STRATEGY

Buying the put gives you the right to sell stock at strike price B. Selling the two puts gives you the obligation to buy stock at strike price A if the options are assigned.

This play enables you to purchase a put that is at-the-money or slightly out-of-the-money without paying full price. The goal is to obtain the put with strike B for a credit or a very small debit by selling the two puts with strike A.

Ideally, you want a slight dip in stock price to strike A. But watch out. Although one of the puts you sold is "covered" by the put you buy with strike B, the second put you sold is "uncovered," exposing you to significant downside risk.

If the stock goes too low, you'll be in for a world of hurt. So beware of any abnormal moves in stock price and have a stop-loss plan in place.

👤 OPTIONS GUY'S TIPS:

☞ Some investors may wish to run this play using index options rather than options on individual stocks. That's because historically, indexes have not been as volatile as individual stocks. Fluctuations in an index's component stock prices tend to cancel one another out, lessening the volatility of the index as a whole.

☞ The maximum value of a front spread is usually achieved when it's close to expiration. You may wish to consider running this play shorter-term; e.g., 30–45 days from expiration.

-0- BREAK-EVEN AT EXPIRATION

If established for a net debit, there are two break-even points:

• Strike B minus the net debit paid to establish the position.

• Strike A minus the maximum profit potential.

If established for a net credit, there is only one break-even point:

• Strike A minus the maximum profit potential.

$ THE SWEET SPOT

You want the stock price exactly at strike A at expiration.

⬆ MAXIMUM POTENTIAL PROFIT

If established for a net debit, potential profit is limited to the difference between strike A and strike B, minus the net debit paid.

If established for a net credit, potential profit is limited to the difference between strike A and strike B plus the net credit.

⬇ MAXIMUM POTENTIAL LOSS

If established for a net debit:

• Risk is limited to the net debit paid if the stock price goes up.

• Risk is substantial but limited to strike A plus the net debit paid if the stock goes to zero.

If established for a net credit:

• Risk is substantial but limited to strike A minus the net credit if the stock goes to zero.

% MARGIN REQUIREMENT

See Appendix A for margin requirement.

✦ AS TIME GOES BY

For this play, time decay is your friend. It's eroding the value of the option you purchased (bad). However, that will be outweighed by the decrease in value of the two options you sold (good).

✦ IMPLIED VOLATILITY

After the play is established, in general you want implied volatility to go down. That's because it will decrease the value of the two options you sold more than the single option you bought.

The closer the stock price is to strike A, the more you want implied volatility to decrease for two reasons. First, it will decrease the value of the near-the-money options you sold at strike A more than the in-the-money option you bought at strike B. Second, it suggests a decreased probability of a wide price swing, whereas you want the stock price to remain stable at or around strike A.

✓ CHECK YOUR PLAY WITH TRADEKING TOOLS

• Use the *Profit + Loss Calculator* to establish break-even points, evaluate how your strategy might change as expiration approaches, and analyze the Greeks.

BACK SPREAD W/ CALLS

AKA Ratio Volatility Spread; Pay Later Call

THE SETUP

- Sell a call, strike price A

- Buy two calls, strike price B

- Generally, the stock will be at or around strike price A

NOTE: Both options have the same expiration month.

WHO SHOULD RUN IT

Seasoned Veterans and higher

WHEN TO RUN IT

 You're extremely bullish on a highly volatile stock.

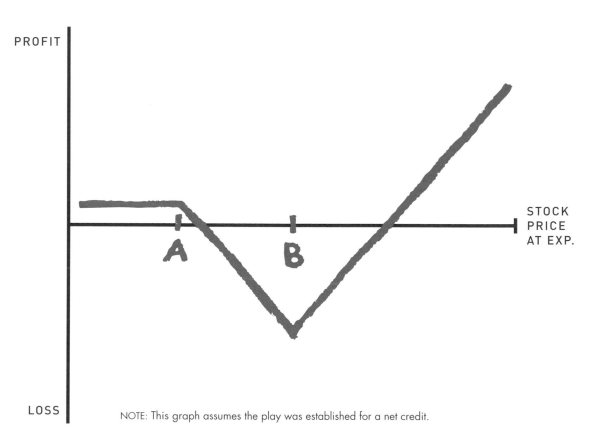

NOTE: This graph assumes the play was established for a net credit.

THE STRATEGY

This is an interesting and unusual play. Essentially, you're selling an at-the-money short call spread (play twelve) in order to help pay for the extra out-of-the-money long call at strike B.

Ideally, you want to establish this play for a small net credit whenever possible. That way, if you're dead wrong and the stock makes a bearish move, you can still make a small profit. However, it may be necessary to establish it for a small net debit, depending on market conditions, days to expiration and the distance between strikes A and B.

Ideally, it would be nice to run this play using longer-term options to give the stock more time to move. However, the marketplace isn't stupid. It knows that to be the case. So the further you go out in time, the more likely it is that you will have to establish the play for a debit.

In addition, the further the strikes are apart, the easier it will be to establish the play for a credit. But as always, there's a tradeoff. Increasing the distance between strike prices also increases your risk, because the stock will have to make a bigger move to the upside to avoid a loss.

Notice that the Profit + Loss graph at expiration looks quite ugly. If the stock only makes a small move to the upside by expiration, you will suffer your maximum loss. However, this is only the risk profile at expiration.

After the play is established, if the stock moves to strike B in the short term, this trade may actually be profitable if implied volatility increases. But if it hangs around there too long, time decay will start to hurt the position. You generally need the stock to continue making a bullish move well past strike B prior to expiration in order for this trade to be profitable.

🧑 OPTIONS GUY'S TIP:

☞ This is a trade you might want to consider just prior to a major news event. Examples might include an announcement regarding FDA approval of a "miracle drug" on a pharmaceutical stock, the outcome of a major legal case, or a pending patent approval.

⓿ BREAK-EVEN AT EXPIRATION

If established for a net debit, the break-even point is equal to strike B plus the maximum risk (strike B minus strike A plus the net debit paid).

If established for a net credit, there are two break-even points for this play:

• Strike A plus the net credit received

• Strike B plus the maximum risk (strike B minus strike A minus the net credit received)

💲 THE SWEET SPOT

The stock goes through the roof.

⬆ MAXIMUM POTENTIAL PROFIT

There's a theoretically unlimited profit potential if the stock goes to infinity. But since the real world doesn't always operate like a theoretical one, let's just say "a lot."

⬇ MAXIMUM POTENTIAL LOSS

Risk is limited to strike B minus strike A, minus the net credit received or plus the net debit paid.

% MARGIN REQUIREMENT

See Appendix A for margin requirement.

🕐 AS TIME GOES BY

The net effect of time decay depends on where the stock is relative to the strike prices and whether or not you've established the play for a net credit or debit.

If the play was established for a net credit:

Time decay is your enemy if the stock is at or above strike A, because it will erode the value of your two long calls more than the value of the short call. Time decay will do the most damage if the stock is at or around strike B, because that's where your maximum loss will occur at expiration.

If the stock is below strike A, time decay is your friend. You want all of the options to expire worthless so you can capture the small credit received.

If the play was established for a net debit:

Time decay is the enemy at stock prices across the board because it will erode the value of your two long calls more than the value of the short one.

CONTINUED ON NEXT PAGE

⊕ IMPLIED VOLATILITY

After the play is established, an increase in implied volatility is almost always good. Although it will increase the value of the option you sold (bad), it will also increase the value of the two options you bought (good). Furthermore, an increase in implied volatility suggests the possibility of a wide price swing.

The exception to this rule is if you established the play for a net credit and the stock price is below strike A. In that case, you may want volatility to decrease so the entire spread expires worthless and you get to keep the small credit.

✓ CHECK YOUR PLAY WITH TRADEKING TOOLS

• Use TradeKing's **Profit + Loss Calculator** to establish break-even points, evaluate how your strategy might change as expiration approaches, and analyze the Greeks.

• Use the **Probability Calculator** to determine the likelihood that the stock might make a large enough move to make this play profitable.

• Use the **Technical Analysis Tool** to look for bullish indicators.

BACK SPREAD W/ PUTS

AKA Ratio Volatility Spread; Pay Later Put

THE SETUP

- Sell a put, strike price B

- Buy two puts, strike price A

- Generally, the stock will be at or around strike price B

NOTE: Both options have the same expiration month.

WHO SHOULD RUN IT

Seasoned Veterans and higher

WHEN TO RUN IT

 You're extremely bearish on a highly volatile stock.

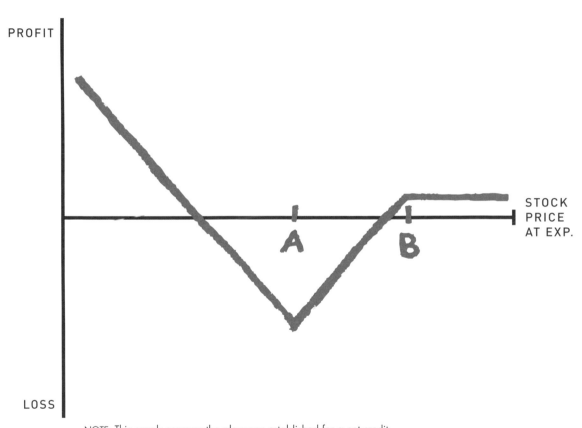

NOTE: This graph assumes the play was established for a net credit.

THE STRATEGY

This is an interesting and unusual play. Essentially, you're selling an at-the-money short put spread (play thirteen) in order to help pay for the extra out-of-the-money long put at strike A.

Ideally, you want to establish this play for a small net credit whenever possible. That way, if you're dead wrong and the stock makes a bullish move, you can still make a small profit. However, it may be necessary to establish it for a small net debit, depending on market conditions, days to expiration and the distance between strikes B and A.

Ideally, it would be nice to run this play using longer-term options to give the stock more time to move. However, the marketplace isn't stupid. It knows that to be the case. So the further you go out in time, the more likely it is that you will have to establish the play for a debit.

In addition, the further the strikes are apart, the easier it will be to establish the play for a credit. But as always, there's a tradeoff. Increasing the distance between strike prices also increases your risk, because the stock will have to make a bigger move to the downside to avoid a loss.

Notice that the Profit + Loss graph at expiration looks quite ugly. If the stock only makes a small move to the downside by expiration, you will suffer your maximum loss. However, this is only the risk profile at expiration.

After the play is established, if the stock moves to strike A in the short term, this trade may actually be profitable if implied volatility increases. But if it hangs around there too long, time decay will start to hurt the position. You generally need the stock to continue making a bearish move well past strike A prior to expiration in order for this trade to be profitable.

👤 OPTIONS GUY'S TIPS:

☞ If you own a volatile stock, this is a potential way to protect your investment against a large downturn with a smaller cash outlay than it would take to purchase a put outright for protection.

☞ This is a trade you might want to consider just prior to a major news event if you expect the outcome to be negative. Examples include pending FDA rejection of a "miracle drug" on a pharmaceutical stock or a bad outcome from a major legal case. A real-life example of when this play might have made sense was in the banking sector during the sub-prime mortgage crisis of 2008.

⊕ BREAK-EVEN AT EXPIRATION

If established for a net debit, the break-even point is strike A minus the maximum risk (strike B minus strike A plus the net debit paid).

If established for a net credit, there are two break-even points for this play:

• Strike A minus the maximum risk (strike B minus strike A minus the net credit received)

• Strike B minus the net credit received

💲 THE SWEET SPOT

You want the stock to completely tank.

⬆ MAXIMUM POTENTIAL PROFIT

There is a substantial profit potential if the stock goes to zero. But keep in mind stocks don't go to zero very often. Choose your stock wisely and be realistic.

⬇ MAXIMUM POTENTIAL LOSS

Risk is limited to strike B minus strike A, minus the net credit received or plus the net debit paid.

％ MARGIN REQUIREMENT

See Appendix A for margin requirement.

⏱ AS TIME GOES BY

The net effect of time decay depends on where the stock is relative to the strike prices and whether or not you've established the play for a net credit or debit.

If the play was established for a net credit:

Time decay is your enemy if the stock is below strike B, because it will erode the value of your two long puts more than the value of the short put. Time decay will do the most damage if the stock is at or around strike A, because that's where your maximum loss will occur at expiration.

If the stock is at or above strike B, time decay is your friend. You want all of the options to expire worthless so you can capture the small credit received.

If the play was established for a net debit:

Time decay is the enemy at stock prices across the board, because it will erode the value of your two long puts more than the value of the short one.

⊕ IMPLIED VOLATILITY

After the play is established, an increase in implied volatility is almost always good. Although it will increase the value of the option you sold (bad), it will also increase the value of the two options you bought (good). Furthermore, an increase in implied volatility suggests the possibility of a wide price swing.

The exception to this rule is if you established the play for a net credit and the stock price is above strike B. In that case, you may want volatility to decrease so the entire spread expires worthless and you get to keep the small credit.

✅ CHECK YOUR PLAY WITH TRADEKING TOOLS

• Use TradeKing's **Profit + Loss Calculator** to establish break-even points, evaluate how your strategy might change as expiration approaches, and analyze the Greeks.

• Use the **Probability Calculator** to see how likely it is that the stock will reach your target price.

• Use the **Technical Analysis Tool** to look for bearish indicators.

LONG CALENDAR SPREAD W/ CALLS

AKA Time Spread; Horizontal Spread

THE SETUP

- Sell a call, strike price A
(near-term expiration – "front-month")

- Buy a call, strike price A
(with expiration one month later – "back-month")

- Generally, the stock will be at or around strike A

WHO SHOULD RUN IT

Seasoned Veterans and higher

NOTE: The level of knowledge required for this trade is considerable, because you're dealing with options that expire on different dates.

WHEN TO RUN IT

 You're anticipating minimal movement on the stock within a specific time frame.

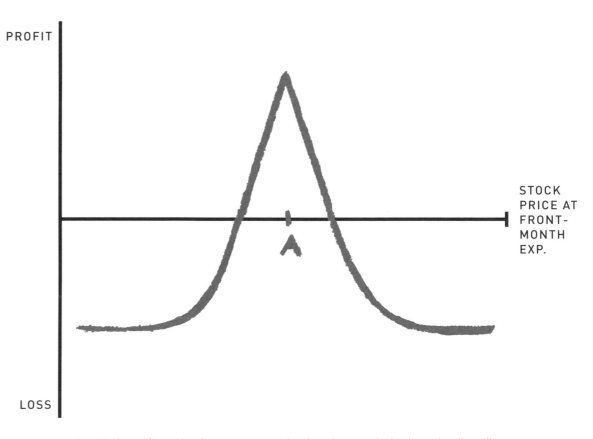

NOTE: The profit and loss lines are not straight. That's because the back-month call is still open when the front-month call expires. Straight lines and hard angles usually indicate that all options in the play have the same expiration date.

THE STRATEGY

When running a calendar spread with calls, you're selling and buying a call with the same strike price, but the call you buy will have a later expiration date than the call you sell. You're taking advantage of accelerating time decay on the front-month (shorter-term) call as expiration approaches. Just before front-month expiration, you want to buy back the shorter-term call for next to nothing. At the same time, you will sell the back-month call to close your position. Ideally, the back-month call will still have significant time value.

If you're anticipating minimal movement on the stock, construct your calendar spread with at-the-money calls. If you're mildly bullish, use slightly out-of-the-money calls. This can give you a lower up-front cost.

Because the front-month and back-month options both have the same strike price, you can't capture any intrinsic value on the options. You can only capture time value. However, as the calls get deep in-the-money or far out-of-the-money, time value will begin to disappear. Time value is maximized with at-the-money options, so you need the stock price to stay as close to strike A as possible.

For this playbook, I'm using the example of a one-month calendar spread. But please note it is possible to use different time intervals. If you're going to use more than a one-month interval between the front-month and back-month options, you need to understand the ins and outs of "rolling." (See the "How We Roll" section of this book.)

👤 OPTIONS GUY'S TIPS:

☞ When establishing one-month calendar spreads, you may wish to consider a "risk one to make two" philosophy. That is, for every net debit of $1 at initiation, you're hoping to receive $2 when closing the position. Use TradeKing's **Profit + Loss Calculator** to estimate whether this seems possible.

☞ To run this play, you need to know how to manage the risk of early assignment on your short options. So be sure to read "What Is Early Exercise and Assignment and Why Does It Happen?" on P.140.

⓿ BREAK-EVEN AT EXPIRATION

It is possible to approximate break-even points, but there are too many variables to give an exact formula.

Because there are two expiration dates for the options in a calendar spread, a pricing model must be used to "guesstimate" what the value of the back-month call will be when the front-month call expires. TradeKing's **Profit + Loss Calculator** can help you in this regard. But keep in mind, the **Profit + Loss Calculator** assumes that all other variables, such as implied volatility, interest rates, etc., remain constant over the life of the trade – and they may not behave that way in reality.

💲 THE SWEET SPOT

You want the stock price to be at strike A when the front-month option expires.

⬆ MAXIMUM POTENTIAL PROFIT

Potential profit is limited to the premium received for the back-month call minus the cost to buy back the front-month call, minus the net debit paid to establish the position.

⬇ MAXIMUM POTENTIAL LOSS

Limited to the net debit paid to establish the trade.

NOTE: You can't precisely calculate your risk at initiation of this play, because it depends on how the back-month call performs.

％ MARGIN REQUIREMENT

After the trade is paid for, no additional margin is required if the position is closed at expiration of the front-month option.

CONTINUED **ON NEXT PAGE**

⏱ AS TIME GOES BY

For this play, time decay is your friend. Because time decay accelerates close to expiration, the front-month call will lose value faster than the back-month call.

✛ IMPLIED VOLATILITY

After the play is established, although you don't want the stock to move much, you're better off if implied volatility increases close to front-month expiration. That will cause the back-month call price to increase, while having little effect on the price of the front-month option. (Near expiration, there is hardly any time value for implied volatility to mess with.)

✓ CHECK YOUR PLAY WITH TRADEKING TOOLS

• Use the **Profit + Loss Calculator** to estimate break-even points, evaluate how your strategy might change as expiration approaches, and analyze the Greeks.

• Use the **Profit + Loss Calculator** to estimate profit potential by determining what the back-month option will be trading for at the expiration of the front month.

LONG CALENDAR SPREAD W/ PUTS

AKA Time Spread; Horizontal Spread

THE SETUP

• Sell a put, strike price A
(near-term expiration – "front-month")

• Buy a put, strike price A
(with expiration one month later – "back-month")

• Generally, the stock will be at or around strike A

WHO SHOULD RUN IT

Seasoned Veterans and higher

NOTE: The level of knowledge required for this trade is considerable, because you're dealing with options that expire on different dates.

WHEN TO RUN IT

 You're anticipating minimal movement on the stock within a specific time frame.

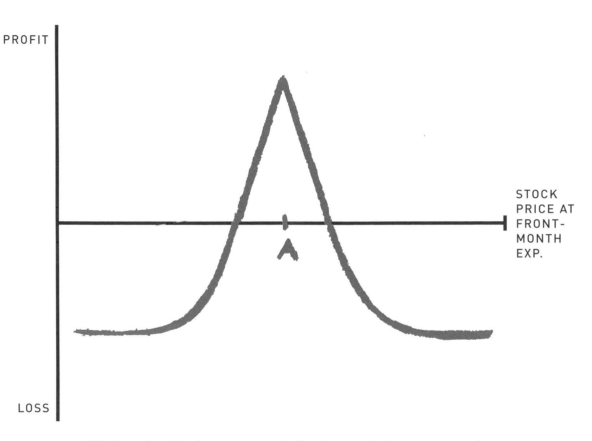

NOTE: The profit and loss lines are not straight. That's because the back-month put is still open when the front-month put expires. Straight lines and hard angles usually indicate that all options in the play have the same expiration date.

THE STRATEGY

When running a calendar spread with puts, you're selling and buying a put with the same strike price, but the put you buy will have a later expiration date than the put you sell. You're taking advantage of accelerating time decay on the front-month (shorter-term) put as expiration approaches. Just before front-month expiration, you want to buy back the shorter-term put for next to nothing. At the same time, you will sell the back-month put to close your position. Ideally, the back-month put will still have significant time value.

If you're anticipating minimal movement on the stock, construct your calendar spread with at-the-money puts. If you're mildly bearish, use slightly out-of-the-money puts. This can give you a lower up-front cost.

Because the front-month and back-month options both have the same strike price, you can't capture any intrinsic value. You can only capture time value. However, as the puts get deep in-the-money or far out-of-the-money, time value will begin to disappear. Time value is maximized with at-the-money options, so you need the stock price to stay as close to strike A as possible.

For this playbook, I'm using the example of a one-month calendar spread. But please note it is possible to use different time intervals. If you're going to use more than a one-month interval between the front-month and back-month options, you need to understand the ins and outs of "rolling." (See the "How We Roll" section of this book.)

🧑 OPTIONS GUY'S TIPS:

☞ When establishing one-month calendar spreads, you may wish to consider a "risk one to make two" philosophy. That is, for every net debit of $1 at initiation, you're hoping to receive $2 when closing the position. Use the TradeKing's *Profit + Loss Calculator* to estimate whether this seems possible.

☞ To run this play, you need to know how to manage the risk of early assignment on your short options. So be sure to read, "What Is Early Exercise and Assignment and Why Does It Happen?" on P.142.

⓿ BREAK-EVEN POINT

It is possible to approximate break-even points, but there are too many variables to give an exact formula.

Because there are two expiration dates for the options in a calendar spread, a pricing model must be used to "guesstimate" what the value of the back-month put will be when the front-month put expires. TradeKing's *Profit + Loss Calculator* can help you in this regard. But keep in mind,

the *Profit + Loss Calculator* assumes that all other variables, such as implied volatility, interest rates, etc., remain constant over the life of the trade – and they may not behave that way in reality.

💲 THE SWEET SPOT

You want the stock price to be at strike A when the front-month option expires.

⬆ MAXIMUM POTENTIAL PROFIT

Potential profit is limited to the premium received for the back-month put minus the cost to buy back the front-month put, minus the net debit paid to establish the position.

⬇ MAXIMUM POTENTIAL LOSS

Limited to the net debit paid to establish the trade.

NOTE: You can't precisely calculate your risk at initiation of this play, because it depends on how the back-month put performs.

% MARGIN REQUIREMENT

After the trade is paid for, no additional margin is required if the position is closed at expiration of the front-month option.

CONTINUED ON NEXT PAGE

☣ AS TIME GOES BY

For this play, time decay is your friend. Because time decay accelerates close to expiration, the front-month put will lose value faster than the back-month put.

✛ IMPLIED VOLATILITY

After the play is established, although you don't want the stock to move much, you're better off if implied volatility increases close to front-month expiration. That will cause the back-month put price to increase, while having little effect on the price of the front-month option. (Near expiration, there is hardly any time value for implied volatility to mess with.)

✔ CHECK YOUR PLAY WITH TRADEKING TOOLS

• Use the **Profit + Loss Calculator** to estimate break-even points, evaluate how your strategy might change as expiration approaches, and analyze the Greeks.

• Use the **Profit + Loss Calculator** to estimate profit potential by determining what the back-month option will be trading for at the expiration of the front month.

DIAGONAL SPREAD W/ CALLS

THE SETUP

• Sell an out-of-the-money call, strike price A (approximately 30 days from expiration – "front-month")

• Buy a further out-of-the-money call, strike price B (approximately 60 days from expiration – "back-month")

• At expiration of the front-month call, sell another call with strike A and the same expiration as the back-month call

• Generally, the stock will be below strike A

WHO SHOULD RUN IT

Seasoned Veterans and higher

NOTE: The level of knowledge required for this trade is considerable, because you're dealing with options that expire on different dates.

WHEN TO RUN IT

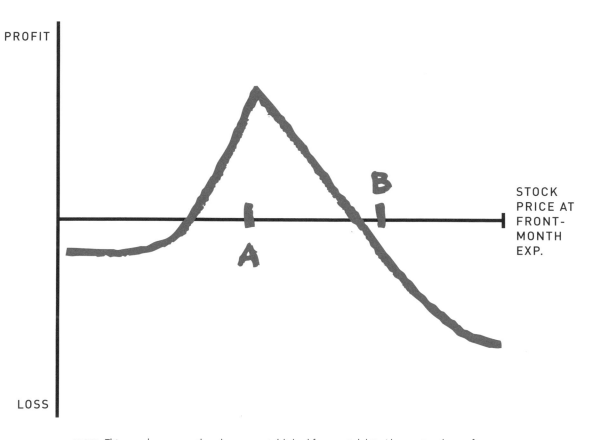

You're expecting neutral activity during the front month, then neutral to bearish activity during the back month.

NOTE: This graph assumes the play was established for a net debit. Also, notice the profit and loss lines are not straight. That's because the back-month call is still open when the front-month call expires. Straight lines and hard angles usually indicate that all options in the play have the same expiration date.

THE STRATEGY

You can think of this as a two-step play. It's a cross between a long calendar spread with calls (play twenty-four) and a short call spread (play twelve). It starts out as a time decay play. Then once you sell a second call with strike A (after front-month expiration), you have legged into a short call spread. Ideally, you will be able to establish this play for a net credit or for a small net debit. Then, the sale of the second call will be all gravy.

For this playbook, I'm using the example of one-month diagonal spreads. But please note, it is possible to use different time intervals. If you're going to use more than a one-month interval between the front-month and back-month options, you need to understand the ins and outs of "rolling." (See "How We Roll" on P.134.)

🙂 OPTIONS GUY'S TIPS:

☛ Ideally, you want some initial volatility with some predictability. Some volatility is good, because the plan is to sell two options, and you want to get as much as possible for them. On the other hand, we want the stock price to remain relatively stable. That's a bit of a paradox, and that's why this play is for more advanced traders.

☛ To run this play, you need to know how to manage the risk of early assignment on your short options. So be sure to read "What Is Early Exercise and Assignment and Why Does It Happen?" on P.140.

⓪ BREAK-EVEN POINTS

It is possible to approximate break-even points, but there are too many variables to give an exact formula.

Because there are two expiration dates for the options in a diagonal spread, a pricing model must be used to "guesstimate" what the value of the back-month call will be when the front-month call expires. TradeKing's *Profit + Loss Calculator* can help you in this regard. But keep in mind, the *Profit + Loss Calculator* assumes that all other variables, such as implied volatility, interest rates, etc., remain constant over the life of the trade – and they may not behave that way in reality.

$ THE SWEET SPOT

For step one, you want the stock price to stay at or around strike A until expiration of the front-month option. For step two, you'll want the stock price to be below strike A when the back-month option expires.

⓵ MAXIMUM POTENTIAL PROFIT

Potential profit is limited to the net credit received for selling both calls with strike A, minus the premium paid for the call with strike B.

NOTE: You can't precisely calculate potential profit at initiation, because it depends on the premium received for the sale of the second call at a later date.

ⓥ MAXIMUM POTENTIAL LOSS

If established for a net credit, risk is limited to the difference between strike A and strike B, minus the net credit received.

If established for a net debit, risk is limited to the difference between strike A and strike B, plus the net debit paid.

NOTE: You can't precisely calculate your risk at initiation, because it depends on the premium received for the sale of the second call at a later date.

% MARGIN REQUIREMENT

See Appendix A for margin requirement.

☀ AS TIME GOES BY

For this play, before front-month expiration, time decay is your friend, since the shorter-term call will lose time value faster than the longer-term call. After closing the front-month call with strike A and selling another call with strike A that has the same expiration as the back-month call with strike B, time decay is somewhat neutral. That's because you'll see erosion in the value of both the option you sold (good) and the option you bought (bad).

CONTINUED **ON NEXT PAGE**

✦ IMPLIED VOLATILITY

After the play is established, although you want neutral movement on the stock if it's at or below Strike A, you're better off if implied volatility increases close to front-month expiration. That way, you will receive a higher premium for selling another call at strike A.

After front-month expiration, you have legged into a short call spread. So the effect of implied volatility depends on where the stock is relative to your strike prices.

If your forecast was correct and the stock price is approaching or below strike A, you want implied volatility to decrease. That's because it will decrease the value of both options, and ideally you want them to expire worthless.

If your forecast was incorrect and the stock price is approaching or above strike B, you want implied volatility to increase for two reasons. First, it will increase the value of the near-the-money option you bought faster than the in-the-money option you sold, thereby decreasing the overall value of the spread. Second, it reflects an increased probability of a price swing (which will hopefully be to the downside).

✔ CHECK YOUR PLAY WITH TRADEKING TOOLS

• Use the *Profit + Loss Calculator* to estimate break-even points, evaluate how your strategy might change as expiration approaches, and analyze the Greeks.

• Use the *Option Pricing Calculator* to "guess-timate" the value of the back-month call you will sell with strike A after closing the front-month call.

DIAGONAL SPREAD W/ PUTS

THE SETUP

• Sell an out-of-the-money put, strike price B (near-term expiration – "front-month")

• Buy a further out-of-the-money put, strike price A (with expiration one month later – "back-month")

• At expiration of the front-month put, sell another put with strike B and the same expiration as the back-month put

• Generally, the stock will be above strike B

WHO SHOULD RUN IT

Seasoned Veterans and higher

NOTE: The level of knowledge required for this trade is considerable, because you're dealing with options that expire on different dates.

WHEN TO RUN IT

 You're expecting neutral activity during the front month, then neutral to bullish activity during the back month.

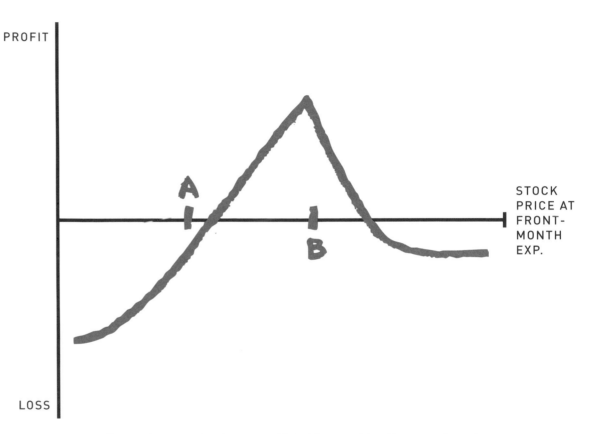

NOTE: This graph assumes the play was established for a net debit. Also, notice the profit and loss lines are not straight. That's because the back-month put is still open when the front-month put expires. Straight lines and hard angles usually indicate that all options in the play have the same expiration date.

THE STRATEGY

You can think of this as a two-step play. It's a cross between a long calendar spread with puts (play twenty-five) and a short put spread (play thirteen). It starts out as a time decay play. Then once you sell a second put with strike B (after front-month expiration), you have legged into a short put spread. Ideally, you will be able to establish this play for a net credit or for a small net debit.

For this playbook, I'm using the example of one-month diagonal spreads. But please note, it is possible to use different time intervals. If you're going to use more than a one-month interval between the front-month and back-month options, you need to understand the ins and outs of "rolling." (See "How We Roll" on P.134.)

👤 OPTIONS GUY'S TIPS:

☞ Ideally, you want some initial volatility with some predictability. Some volatility is good, because the plan is to sell two options, and you want to get as much as possible for them. On the other hand, we want the stock price to remain relatively stable. That's a bit of a paradox, and that's why this play is for more advanced traders.

☞ To run this play, you need to know how to manage the risk of early assignment on your short options. So be sure to read "What Is Early Exercise and Assignment and Why Does It Happen?" on P.140.

🔟 BREAK-EVEN POINTS

It is possible to approximate break-even points, but there are too many variables to give an exact formula.

Because there are two expiration dates for the options in a diagonal spread, a pricing model must be used to "guesstimate" what the value of the back-month put will be when the front-month put expires. TradeKing's *Profit + Loss Calculator* can help you in this regard. But keep in mind, the *Profit + Loss Calculator* assumes that all other variables, such as implied volatility, interest rates, etc., remain constant over the life of the trade – and they may not behave that way in reality.

💲 THE SWEET SPOT

For step one, you want the stock price to stay at or around strike B until expiration of the front-month option. For step two, you'll want the stock price to be above strike B when the back-month option expires.

⬆️ MAXIMUM POTENTIAL PROFIT

Profit is limited to the net credit received for selling both puts with strike B, minus the premium paid for the put with strike A.

NOTE: You can't precisely calculate potential profit at initiation, because it depends on the premium received for the sale of the second put at a later date.

⬇️ MAXIMUM POTENTIAL LOSS

If established for a net credit, risk is limited to the difference between strike A and strike B, minus the net credit received.

If established for a net debit, risk is limited to the difference between strike A and strike B, plus the net debit paid.

NOTE: You can't precisely calculate your risk at initiation, because it depends on the premium received for the sale of the second put at a later date.

% MARGIN REQUIREMENT

See Appendix A for margin requirement.

⏱️ AS TIME GOES BY

For this play, before front-month expiration, time decay is your friend, since the shorter-term put will lose time value faster than the longer-term put. After closing the front-month put with strike B and selling another put with strike B that has the same expiration as the back-month put with strike A, time decay is somewhat neutral. That's because you'll see erosion in the value of both the option you sold (good) and the option you bought (bad).

IMPLIED VOLATILITY

After the play is established, although you want neutral movement on the stock if it's at or above strike B, you're better off if implied volatility increases close to front-month expiration. That way, you will receive a higher premium for selling another put at strike B.

After front-month expiration, you have legged into a short put spread. So the effect of implied volatility depends on where the stock is relative to your strike prices.

If your forecast was correct and the stock price is approaching or above strike B, you want implied volatility to decrease. That's because it will decrease the value of both options, and ideally you want them to expire worthless.

If your forecast was incorrect and the stock price is approaching or below strike A, you want implied volatility to increase for two reasons. First, it will increase the value of the near-the-money option you bought faster than the in-the-money option you sold, thereby decreasing the overall value of the spread. Second, it reflects an increased probability of a price swing (which will hopefully be to the upside).

CHECK YOUR PLAY WITH TRADEKING TOOLS

• Use the *Profit + Loss Calculator* to estimate break-even points, evaluate how your strategy might change as expiration approaches, and analyze the Greeks.

• Use the *Option Pricing Calculator* to "guess-timate" the value of the back-month call you will sell at strike B after closing the front-month put.

LONG BUTTERFLY SPREAD W/ CALLS

THE SETUP

- Buy a call, strike price A
- Sell two calls, strike price B
- Buy a call, strike price C
- Generally, the stock will be at strike B

NOTE: Strike prices are equidistant, and all options have the same expiration month.

WHO SHOULD RUN IT

Seasoned Veterans and higher

NOTE: Due to the narrow sweet spot and the fact you're trading three different options in one play, butterfly spreads may be better suited for more advanced option traders.

WHEN TO RUN IT

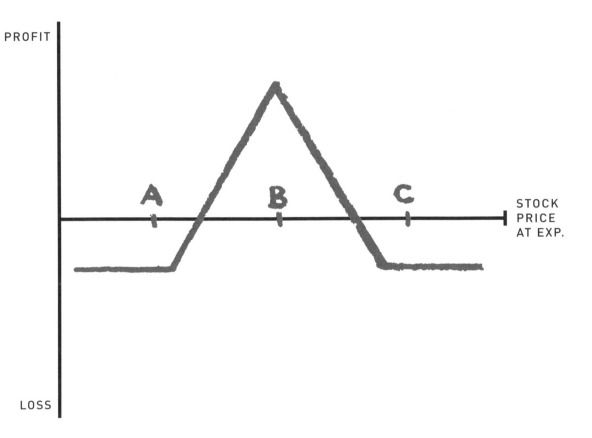

(N) Typically, investors will use butterfly spreads when anticipating minimal movement on the stock within a specific time frame.

THE STRATEGY

A long butterfly spread with calls is a combination of a long call spread (play ten) and a short call spread (play twelve), with the spreads converging at strike price B.

Ideally, you want the calls with strikes B and C to expire worthless while capturing the intrinsic value of the in-the-money call with strike A.

Because you're selling the two options with strike B, butterflies are a relatively low-cost strategy. So the risk vs. reward can be tempting. However, the odds of hitting the sweet spot are fairly low.

Constructing your butterfly spread with strike B slightly in-the-money or slightly out-of-the-money may make it a bit less expensive to run. This will put a directional bias on the trade. If strike B is higher than the stock price, this would be considered a bullish trade. If strike B is below the stock price, it would be a bearish trade. (But for simplicity's sake, if bearish, puts would usually be used to construct the spread.)

👤 OPTIONS GUY'S TIP:

☞ Some investors may wish to run this play using index options rather than options on individual stocks. That's because historically, indexes have not been as volatile as individual stocks. Fluctuations in an index's component stock prices tend to cancel one another out, lessening the volatility of the index as a whole.

🔟 BREAK-EVEN AT EXPIRATION

There are two break-even points for this play:

- Strike A plus the net debit paid.
- Strike C minus the net debit paid.

💲 THE SWEET SPOT

You want the stock price to be exactly at strike B at expiration.

⬆ MAXIMUM POTENTIAL PROFIT

Potential profit is limited to strike B minus strike A minus the net debit paid.

⬇ MAXIMUM POTENTIAL LOSS

Risk is limited to the net debit paid.

% MARGIN REQUIREMENT

After the trade is paid for, no additional margin is required.

🕐 AS TIME GOES BY

For this play, time decay is your friend. Ideally, you want all options except the call with strike A to expire worthless with the stock precisely at strike B.

⚡ IMPLIED VOLATILITY

After the play is established, the effect of implied volatility depends on where the stock is relative to your strike prices.

If your forecast was correct and the stock price is at or around strike B, you want volatility to decrease. Your main concern is the two options you sold at strike B. A decrease in implied volatility will cause those near-the-money options to decrease in value, thereby increasing the overall value of the butterfly. In addition, you want the stock price to remain stable around strike B, and a decrease in implied volatility suggests that may be the case.

If your forecast was incorrect and the stock price is approaching or outside of strike A or C, in general you want volatility to increase, especially as expiration approaches. An increase in volatility will increase the value of the option you own at the near-the-money strike, while having less effect on the short options at strike B, thereby increasing the overall value of the butterfly.

✓ CHECK YOUR PLAY WITH TRADEKING TOOLS

- Use the *Profit + Loss Calculator* to establish break-even points, evaluate how your strategy might change as expiration approaches, and analyze the Greeks.

LONG BUTTERFLY SPREAD W/ PUTS

THE SETUP

- Buy a put, strike price A
- Sell two puts, strike price B
- Buy a put, strike price C
- Generally, the stock will be at strike B

NOTE: Strike prices are equidistant, and all options have the same expiration month.

WHO SHOULD RUN IT

Seasoned Veterans and higher

NOTE: Due to the narrow sweet spot and the fact you're trading three different options in one play, butterfly spreads may be better suited for more advanced option traders.

WHEN TO RUN IT

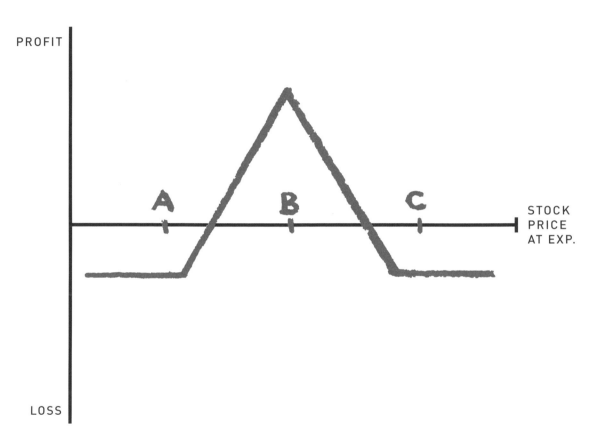

(N) Typically, investors will use butterfly spreads when anticipating minimal movement on the stock within a specific time frame.

THE STRATEGY

A long butterfly spread with puts is a combination of a short put spread (play thirteen) and a long put spread (play eleven), with the spreads converging at strike B.

Ideally, you want the puts with strikes A and B to expire worthless, while capturing the intrinsic value of the in-the-money put with strike C.

Because you're selling two options with strike B, butterflies are a relatively low-cost strategy. So the risk vs. reward can be tempting. However, the odds of hitting the sweet spot are fairly low.

Constructing your butterfly spread with strike B slightly in-the-money or slightly out-of-the-money may make it a bit less expensive to run. This will put a directional bias on the trade. If strike B is higher than the stock price, this would be considered a bullish trade. If strike B is below the stock price, it would be a bearish trade. (But for simplicity's sake, if bullish, calls would usually be used to construct the spread.)

👤 OPTIONS GUY'S TIP:

☛ Some investors may wish to run this play using index options rather than options on individual stocks. That's because historically, indexes have not been as volatile as individual stocks. Fluctuations in an index's component stock prices tend to cancel one another out, lessening the volatility of the index as a whole.

⓪ BREAK-EVEN AT EXPIRATION

There are two break-even points for this play:

- Strike A plus the net debit paid.
- Strike C minus the net debit paid.

💲 THE SWEET SPOT

You want the stock price to be exactly at strike B at expiration.

⬆ MAXIMUM POTENTIAL PROFIT

Potential profit is limited to strike C minus strike B minus the net debit paid.

⬇ MAXIMUM POTENTIAL LOSS

Risk is limited to the net debit paid.

﹪ MARGIN REQUIREMENT

After the trade is paid for, no additional margin is required.

☻ AS TIME GOES BY

For this play, time decay is your friend. Ideally, you want all options except the put with strike C to expire worthless with the stock precisely at strike B.

⊕ IMPLIED VOLATILITY

After the play is established, the effect of implied volatility depends on where the stock is relative to your strike prices.

If your forecast was correct and the stock price is at or around strike B, you want volatility to decrease. Your main concern is the two options you sold at strike B. A decrease in implied volatility will cause those near-the-money options to decrease in value, thereby increasing the overall value of the butterfly. In addition, you want the stock price to remain stable around strike B, and a decrease in implied volatility suggests that may be the case.

If your forecast was incorrect and the stock price is approaching or outside of strike A or C, in general you want volatility to increase, especially as expiration approaches. An increase in volatility will increase the value of the option you own at the near-the-money strike, while having less effect on the short options at strike B, thereby increasing the overall value of the butterfly.

✓ CHECK YOUR PLAY WITH TRADEKING TOOLS

- Use the **Profit + Loss Calculator** to establish break-even points, evaluate how your strategy might change as expiration approaches, and analyze the Greeks.

IRON BUTTERFLY

THE SETUP

- Buy a put, strike price A
- Sell a put, strike price B
- Sell a call, strike price B
- Buy a call, strike price C
- Generally, the stock will be at strike B

NOTE: Strike prices are equidistant, and all options have the same expiration month.

WHO SHOULD RUN IT

Seasoned Veterans and higher

NOTE: Due to the narrow sweet spot and the fact you're trading four different options in one play, iron butterfly spreads may be better suited for more advanced option traders.

WHEN TO RUN IT

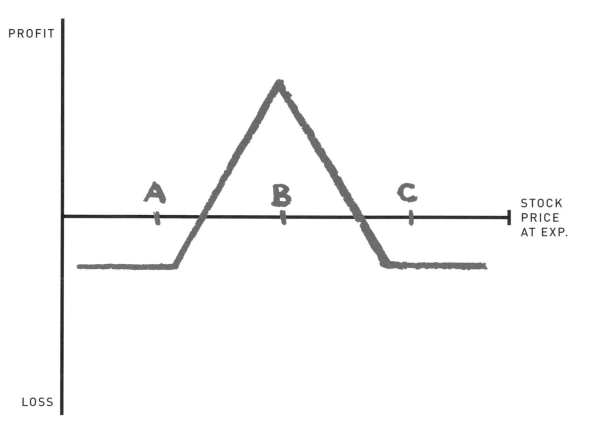

(N) Typically, investors will use butterfly spreads when anticipating minimal movement on the stock within a specific time frame.

THE STRATEGY

You can think of this play as simultaneously running a short put spread (play thirteen) and a short call spread (play twelve) with the spreads converging at strike B. Because it's a combination of short spreads, an iron butterfly can be established for a net credit.

Ideally, you want all of the options in this spread to expire worthless, with the stock at strike B. However, the odds of this happening are fairly low, so you'll probably have to pay something to close your position.

It is possible to put a directional bias on this trade. If strike B is higher than the stock price, this would be considered a bullish trade. If strike B is below the stock price, it would be a bearish trade.

👤 OPTIONS GUY'S TIPS:

☞ Since an iron butterfly is a "four-legged" spread, the commissions typically cost more than a long butterfly. That causes some investors to opt for the long butterfly instead. (However, since TradeKing's commissions are so low, this will hurt you less than it would with some other brokers.)

☞ Some investors may wish to run this play using index options rather than options on individual stocks. That's because historically, indexes have not been as volatile as individual stocks. Fluctuations in an index's component stock prices tend to cancel one another out, lessening the volatility of the index as a whole.

🔟 BREAK-EVEN AT EXPIRATION

There are two break-even points for this play:

- Strike B plus net credit received.
- Strike B minus net credit received.

💲 THE SWEET SPOT

You want the stock price to be exactly at strike B at expiration so all four options expire worthless.

⬆ MAXIMUM POTENTIAL PROFIT

Potential profit is limited to the net credit received.

⬇ MAXIMUM POTENTIAL LOSS

Risk is limited to strike B minus strike A, minus the net credit received when establishing the position.

% MARGIN REQUIREMENT

See Appendix A for margin requirement.

🕛 AS TIME GOES BY

For this play, time decay is your friend. Ideally, you want all of the options in this spread to expire worthless with the stock precisely at strike B.

〽 IMPLIED VOLATILITY

After the play is established, the effect of implied volatility depends on where the stock is relative to your strike prices.

If your forecast was correct and the stock price is at or around strike B, you want volatility to decrease. Your main concern is the two options you sold at strike B. A decrease in implied volatility will cause those near-the-money options to decrease in value. So the overall value of the butterfly will decrease, making it less expensive to close your position. In addition, you want the stock price to remain stable around strike B, and a decrease in implied volatility suggests that may be the case.

If your forecast was incorrect and the stock price is below strike A or above strike C, in general you want volatility to increase. This is especially true as expiration approaches. An increase in volatility will increase the value of the option you own at the near-the-money strike, while having less effect on the short options at strike B. So the overall value of the iron butterfly will decrease, making it less expensive to close your position.

✅ CHECK YOUR PLAY WITH TRADEKING TOOLS

- Use the **Profit + Loss Calculator** to establish break-even points, evaluate how your strategy might change as expiration approaches, and analyze the Greeks.

SKIP STRIKE BUTTERFLY W/ CALLS

AKA Broken Wing Butterfly; Split Strike Butterfly

THE SETUP

- Buy a call, strike price A
- Sell two calls, strike price B
- Skip over strike price C
- Buy a call, strike price D
- Generally, the stock will be at or below strike A

NOTE: Strike prices are equidistant, and all options have the same expiration month.

WHO SHOULD RUN IT

Seasoned Veterans and higher

NOTE: Due to the narrow sweet spot and the fact you're trading four different options in one play, skip strike butterflies may be better suited for more advanced option traders.

WHEN TO RUN IT

 You're slightly bullish. You want the stock to rise to strike B and then stop.

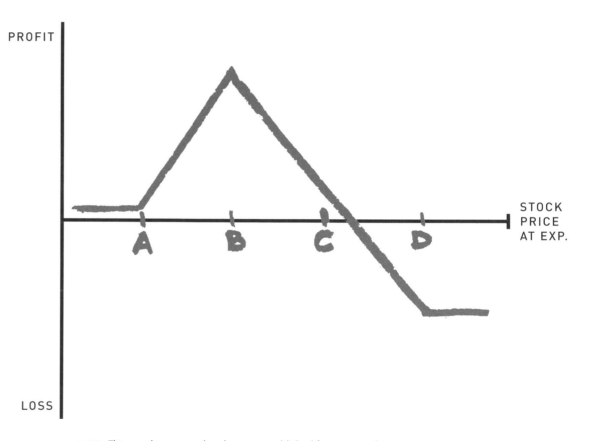

NOTE: This graph assumes the play was established for a net credit.

THE STRATEGY

You can think of this play as embedding a short call spread (play twelve) inside a long butterfly spread with calls (play twenty-eight). Essentially, you're selling the short call spread to help pay for the butterfly. Because establishing those spreads separately would entail both buying and selling a call with strike C, they cancel each other out and it becomes a dead strike.

The embedded short call spread makes it possible to establish this play for a net credit or a relatively small net debit. However, due to the addition of the short call spread, there is more risk than with a traditional butterfly.

A skip strike butterfly with calls is more of a directional play than a standard butterfly. Ideally, you want the stock price to increase somewhat, but not beyond strike B. In this case, the calls with strikes B and D will approach zero, but you'll retain the premium for the call with strike A.

This play is usually run with the stock price at or around strike A. That helps manage the risk, because the stock will have to make a significant move upward before you encounter the maximum loss.

👤 OPTIONS GUY'S TIP:

☞ Some investors may wish to run this play using index options rather than options on individual stocks. That's because historically, indexes have not been as volatile as individual stocks. Fluctuations in an index's component stock prices tend to cancel one another out, lessening the volatility of the index as a whole.

🔟 BREAK-EVEN AT EXPIRATION

If established for a net credit (as in the graph at left) then the break-even point is strike C plus the net credit received when establishing the play.

If established for a net debit, then there are two break-even points:

- Strike A plus net debit paid.
- Strike C minus net debit paid.

💲 THE SWEET SPOT

You want the stock price to be exactly at strike B at expiration.

⬆️ MAXIMUM POTENTIAL PROFIT

Potential profit is limited to strike B minus strike A minus the net debit paid, or plus the net credit received.

⬇️ MAXIMUM POTENTIAL LOSS

Risk is limited to the difference between strike C and strike D minus the net credit received or plus the net debit paid.

% MARGIN REQUIREMENT

See Appendix A for margin requirement.

✴️ AS TIME GOES BY

For this play, time decay is your friend. Ideally, you want all options except the call with strike A to expire worthless.

⟐ IMPLIED VOLATILITY

After the play is established, the effect of implied volatility depends on where the stock is relative to your strike prices.

If the stock is at or near strike B, you want volatility to decrease. Your main concern is the two options you sold at strike B. A decrease in implied volatility will cause those near-the-money options to decrease in value, thereby increasing the overall value of the butterfly. In addition, you want the stock price to remain stable around strike B, and a decrease in implied volatility suggests that may be the case.

If the stock price is approaching or outside strike A or D, in general you want volatility to increase. An increase in volatility will increase the value of the option you own at the near-the-money strike, while having less effect on the short options at strike B.

✅ CHECK YOUR PLAY WITH TRADEKING TOOLS

- Use the *Profit + Loss Calculator* to establish break-even points, evaluate how your strategy might change as expiration approaches, and analyze the Greeks.

- When using this as a bullish play, use the *Technical Analysis Tool* to look for directional indicators.

SKIP STRIKE BUTTERFLY W/ PUTS

AKA Broken Wing Butterfly; Split Strike Butterfly

THE SETUP

- Buy a put, strike price A
- Skip strike price B
- Sell two puts, strike price C
- Buy a put, strike price D
- Generally, the stock will be at or above strike D

NOTE: Strike prices are equidistant, and all options have the same expiration month.

WHO SHOULD RUN IT

Seasoned Veterans and higher

NOTE: Due to the narrow sweet spot and the fact you're trading four different options in one play, skip strike butterflies may be better suited for more advanced option traders.

WHEN TO RUN IT

 You're slightly bearish. You want the stock to go down to strike C and then stop.

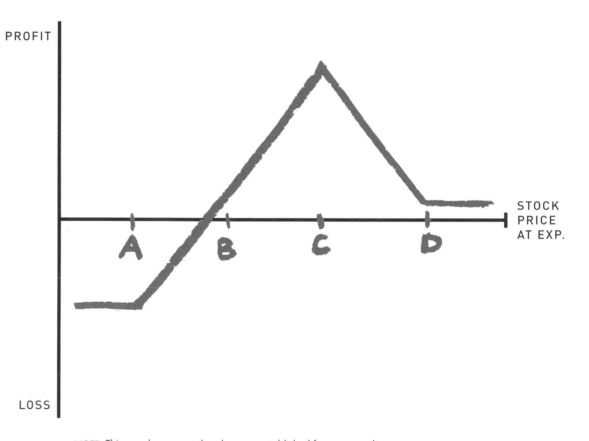

NOTE: This graph assumes the play was established for a net credit.

THE STRATEGY

You can think of this play as embedding a short put spread (play thirteen) inside a long butterfly spread with puts (play twenty-nine). Essentially, you're selling the short put spread to help pay for the butterfly. Because establishing those spreads separately would entail both buying and selling a put with strike B, they cancel each other out and it becomes a dead strike.

The embedded short put spread makes it possible to establish this play for a net credit or a relatively small net debit. However, due to the addition of the short put spread, there is more risk than with a traditional butterfly.

A skip strike butterfly is more of a directional play than a standard butterfly. Ideally, you want the stock price to decrease somewhat, but not beyond strike C. In this case, the puts with strikes A and C will approach zero, but you'll retain the premium for the put with strike D.

This play is usually run with the stock price at or around strike D. That helps manage the risk, because the stock will have to make a significant downward move before you encounter the maximum loss.

👤 OPTIONS GUY'S TIP:

☞ Some investors may wish to run this play using index options rather than options on individual stocks. That's because historically, indexes have not been as volatile as individual stocks. Fluctuations in an index's component stock prices tend to cancel one another out, lessening the volatility of the index as a whole.

⓿ BREAK-EVEN AT EXPIRATION

If established for a net credit (as in the graph at left) then the break-even point is strike B minus the net credit received when establishing the play.

If established for a net debit, then there are two break-even points:

- Strike D minus net debit paid.
- Strike B plus net debit paid.

💲 THE SWEET SPOT

You want the stock price to be exactly at strike C at expiration.

⬆ MAXIMUM POTENTIAL PROFIT

Potential profit is limited to strike D minus strike C minus the net debit paid, or plus the net credit received.

⬇ MAXIMUM POTENTIAL LOSS

Risk is limited to the difference between strike A and strike B, minus the net credit received or plus the net debit paid.

% MARGIN REQUIREMENT

See Appendix A for margin requirement.

☾ AS TIME GOES BY

For this play, time decay is your friend. Ideally, you want all options except the put with strike D to expire worthless.

◈ IMPLIED VOLATILITY

After the play is established, the effect of implied volatility depends on where the stock is relative to your strike prices.

If the stock is at or near strike C, you want volatility to decrease. Your main concern is the two options you sold at strike C. A decrease in implied volatility will cause those near-the-money options to decrease in value, thereby increasing the overall value of the butterfly. In addition, you want the stock price to remain stable around strike C, and a decrease in implied volatility suggests that may be the case.

If the stock price is approaching or outside strike D or A, in general you want volatility to increase. An increase in volatility will increase the value of the option you own at the near-the-money strike, while having less effect on the short options at strike C.

✓ CHECK YOUR PLAY WITH TRADEKING TOOLS

- Use the *Profit + Loss Calculator* to establish break-even points, evaluate how your strategy might change as expiration approaches, and analyze the Greeks.

- When using this as a bearish play, use the *Technical Analysis Tool* to look for directional indicators.

INVERSE SKIP STRIKE BUTTERFLY W/ CALLS

AKA Inverse Broken Wing Butterfly; Inverse Split Strike Butterfly

THE SETUP

- Sell a call with strike price A

- Buy two calls with strike price B

- Skip over strike price C

- Sell a call with strike price D

- Generally, the stock will be at or around strike price A

NOTE: Strike prices are equidistant and all options have the same expiration month.

WHO SHOULD RUN IT

Seasoned Veterans and higher

WHEN TO RUN IT

 You're extremely bullish on a highly volatile stock.

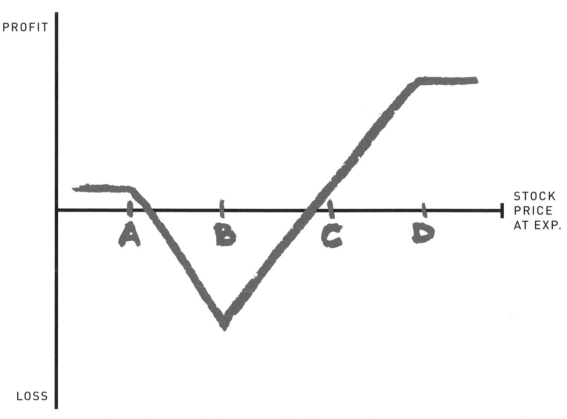

NOTE: This graph assumes the play was established for a net credit.

THE STRATEGY

You can think of this play as a back spread with calls (play twenty-two) with a twist. Instead of simply running a back spread with calls (sell one call, buy two calls), selling the extra call at strike D helps to reduce the overall cost to establish the trade.

Obviously, when running this play, you are expecting an enormous bullish move. So it's a play for extremely volatile times when stocks are more likely to make wide moves in either direction.

When implied volatility rises, in general option prices go up independent of stock price movement. That's why we need some help to pay for the strategy by selling the call at strike D, even though it sets a limit on your potential profit.

Ideally, you want to establish this play for a net credit whenever possible. That way, if you're dead wrong and the stock makes a bearish move, you can still make a small profit. However, it may be necessary to establish it for a small net debit, depending on market conditions, days to expiration and the width between strike prices.

The further the strikes are apart, the easier it will be to establish the play for a credit. But as always, there's a tradeoff. Increasing the distance between strike prices also increases your risk, because the stock will have to make a bigger move to the upside to avoid a loss.

As with back spreads, the Profit + Loss graph for this play looks quite ugly at first glance. If the stock only makes a small move to the upside by expiration, you will suffer your maximum loss.

However, this is only the situation at expiration. When the play is first established, if the stock moves to strike B, this trade may actually be profitable in the short term if implied volatility increases. But if it hangs around strike B too long, time decay will start to hurt the position.

For this to be a profitable trade, you generally need the stock to continue making a bullish move up to or beyond strike D prior to expiration.

👤 OPTIONS GUY'S TIP:

☞ You may wish to consider running this play on stocks with 150% or greater implied volatility on the at-the-money option in the expiration month that you're trading. An example of a stock where this might be the case could be a pharmaceutical company that is awaiting FDA approval of a brand-new "miracle drug," and you expect the outcome to be positive.

⓿ BREAK-EVEN AT EXPIRATION

If established for a net debit, the break-even point is strike C plus the net debit paid.

If established for a net credit, there are two break-even points:

• Strike A plus the net credit received

• Strike C minus the net credit received

💲 THE SWEET SPOT

You want the stock to be at strike price D or higher at expiration.

⬆ MAXIMUM POTENTIAL PROFIT

Potential profit is limited to strike D minus strike C minus the net debit paid, or plus the net credit received.

⬇ MAXIMUM POTENTIAL LOSS

Potential risk is limited to strike B minus strike A plus the net debit paid, or minus the net credit received.

% MARGIN REQUIREMENT

See Appendix A for margin requirement.

✖ AS TIME GOES BY

The net effect of time decay depends on where the stock is relative to the strike prices and whether or not you've established the play for a net credit or debit.

If the play was established for a net credit:

If the stock is below strike A, time decay is your friend. You want all of the options to expire worthless so you can capture the small credit received.

If the stock is between strike A and strike C, time decay is your enemy because your chance to make a profit will be eroding along with the value of your two long calls. Time decay will do the most damage if the stock is at or around strike B, because that's where your maximum loss will occur at expiration.

If the stock moves above strike C toward strike D, time decay becomes your friend again because you need it to erode the value of the short call at that strike to achieve your maximum profit.

If the play was established for a net debit:

If the stock is below strike C, time decay is the enemy because your chance to make a profit will be eroding along with the value of your two long calls.

As the stock moves above strike C and approaches strike D, time decay becomes your friend. You need it to erode the value of the short call at that strike to achieve your maximum profit.

⊕ IMPLIED VOLATILITY

After the play is established, the effect of implied volatility depends on where the stock is relative to your strike prices.

If your forecast is correct and the stock is approaching or above strike D, you want volatility to decrease. A decrease in implied volatility will decrease the value of the short options at strikes A and D and increase the overall value of your position.

If your initial forecast was wrong and the stock has stagnated around strike B, you want implied volatility to increase for two reasons. First, an increase in implied volatility will increase the value of the near-the-money options you bought at strike B more than it will affect the value of the options you sold at strikes A and D. Second, an increase in implied volatility suggests an increased possibility of a larger price swing (hopefully to the upside).

If you established the play for a net credit and the stock price is below strike A, you may want volatility to decrease so the entire spread expires worthless and you get to keep the small credit.

✓ CHECK YOUR PLAY WITH TRADEKING TOOLS

• Use TradeKing's *Profit + Loss Calculator* to establish break-even points, evaluate how your strategy might change as expiration approaches, and analyze the Greeks.

• Use the *Probability Calculator* to determine the likelihood that the stock might make a large enough move to make this play profitable.

• Use the *Technical Analysis Tool* to look for bullish indicators.

INVERSE SKIP STRIKE BUTTERFLY W/ PUTS

AKA Inverse Broken Wing Butterfly; Inverse Split Strike Butterfly

THE SETUP

- Sell a put with strike price D

- Buy two puts with strike price C

- Skip over strike price B

- Sell a put with strike price A

- Generally, the stock will be at or around strike price D

NOTE: Strike prices are equidistant and all options have the same expiration month.

WHO SHOULD RUN IT

Seasoned Veterans and higher

WHEN TO RUN IT

 You're extremely bearish on a highly volatile stock.

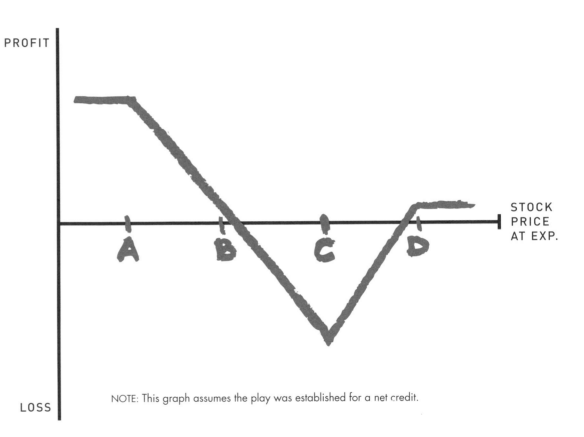

NOTE: This graph assumes the play was established for a net credit.

THE STRATEGY

You can think of this play as a back spread with puts (play twenty-three) with a twist. Instead of simply running a back spread with puts (sell one put, buy two puts), selling the extra put at strike A helps to reduce the overall cost to establish the trade.

Obviously, when running this play, you are expecting an enormous bearish move. So it's a play for extremely volatile times when stocks are more likely to make wide moves in either direction.

When implied volatility rises, in general option prices go up independent of stock price movement. That's why we need some help to pay for the strategy by selling the put at strike A, even though it sets a lower limit on your potential profit.

Ideally, you want to establish this play for a net credit whenever possible. That way, if you're dead wrong and the stock makes a bullish move, you can still make a small profit. However, it may be necessary to establish it for a small net debit, depending on market conditions, days to expiration and the width between strike prices.

The further the strikes are apart, the easier it will be to establish the play for a credit. But as always, there's a tradeoff. Increasing the distance between strike prices also increases your risk, because the stock will have to make a bigger move to the downside to avoid a loss.

As with back spreads, the profit + loss graph for this play looks quite ugly at first glance. If the stock only makes a small move to the downside by expiration, you will suffer your maximum loss.

However, this is only the situation at expiration. When the play is first established, if the stock moves to strike C, this trade may actually be profitable in the short term if implied volatility increases. But if it hangs around strike C too long, time decay will start to hurt the position.

For this to be a profitable trade, you generally need the stock to continue making a bearish move down to or beyond strike A prior to expiration.

👤 OPTIONS GUY'S TIP:

☞ You may wish to consider running this play on stocks with 150% or greater implied volatility on the at-the-money option in the expiration month that you're trading. A real-life example of when this play might have made sense was in the banking sector during the subprime mortgage crisis of 2008.

🔟 BREAK-EVEN AT EXPIRATION

If established for a net debit, the break-even point is strike B minus the net debit paid.

If established for a net credit, there are two break-even points:

• Strike D minus the net credit received

• Strike B plus the net credit received

💲 THE SWEET SPOT

You want the stock to be at strike price A or lower at expiration.

⬆ MAXIMUM POTENTIAL PROFIT

Potential profit is limited to strike B minus strike A minus the net debit paid, or plus the net credit received.

⬇ MAXIMUM POTENTIAL LOSS

Potential risk is limited to strike D minus strike C plus the net debit paid, or minus the net credit received.

% MARGIN REQUIREMENT

See Appendix A for Margin Requirement.

⏱ AS TIME GOES BY

The net effect of time decay depends on where the stock is relative to the strike prices and whether or not you've established the play for a net credit or debit.

If the play was established for a net credit:

If the stock is above strike D, time decay is your friend. You want all of the options to expire worthless so you can capture the small credit received.

If the stock is between strike D and strike B, time decay is your enemy because your chance to make a profit will be eroding along with the value of your two long puts. Time decay will do the most damage if the stock is at or around strike C, because that's where your maximum loss will occur at expiration.

As the stock moves below strike B and approaches strike A, time decay becomes your friend again because you need it to erode the value of the short put at that strike to achieve your maximum profit.

If the play was established for a net debit:

If the stock is above strike B, time decay is the enemy because your chance to make a profit will be eroding along with the value of your two long puts.

As the stock moves below strike B and approaches strike A, time decay becomes your friend. You need it to erode the value of the short call at that strike to achieve your maximum profit.

⊕ IMPLIED VOLATILITY

After the play is established, the effect of implied volatility depends on where the stock is relative to your strike prices.

If your forecast is correct and the stock is approaching or below strike A, you want volatility to decrease. A decrease in implied volatility will decrease the value of the short options at strikes D and A and increase the overall value of your position.

If your initial forecast was wrong and the stock has stagnated around strike C, you want implied volatility to increase for two reasons. First, an increase in implied volatility will increase the value of the near-the-money options you bought at strike C more than it will affect the value of the options you sold at strikes D and A. Second, an increase in implied volatility suggests an increased possibility of a larger price swing (hopefully to the downside).

If you established the play for a net credit and the stock price is above strike D, you may want volatility to decrease so the entire spread expires worthless and you get to keep the small credit.

✓ CHECK YOUR PLAY WITH TRADEKING TOOLS

• Use TradeKing's **Profit + Loss Calculator** to establish break-even points, evaluate how your strategy might change as expiration approaches, and analyze the Greeks.

• Use the **Probability Calculator** to determine the likelihood that the stock might make a large enough move to make this play profitable.

• Use the **Technical Analysis Tool** to look for bearish indicators.

CHRISTMAS TREE BUTTERFLY W/ CALLS

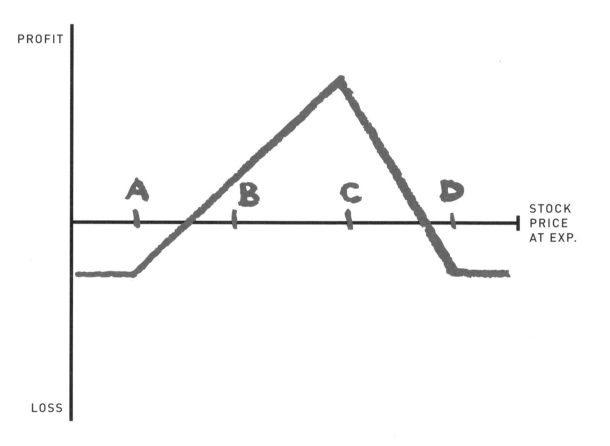

PROFIT

A   B   C   D

STOCK PRICE AT EXP.

LOSS

THE SETUP

- Buy a call, strike price A
- Skip over strike price B
- Sell three calls, strike price C
- Buy two calls, strike price D
- Generally, the stock will be at or around strike A

NOTE: Strike prices are equidistant, and all options have the same expiration month.

WHO SHOULD RUN IT

Seasoned Veterans and higher

WHEN TO RUN IT

 You're slightly bullish. You want the stock to rise to strike C and then stop.

THE STRATEGY

You can think of this play as simultaneously buying one long call spread (play ten) with strikes A and C and selling two short call spreads (play twelve) with strikes C and D. Because the long call spread skips over strike B, the distance between its strikes will be twice as wide as the strikes in the short call spread. In other words, if the width from strike A to strike C is 5.00, the width from strike C to strike D will be 2.50.

Whereas a traditional butterfly with calls (play twenty-eight) is often used as a neutral strategy, this play is usually run with a slightly bullish directional bias. To reach the sweet spot, the stock price needs to increase a bit.

Selling two short call spreads with half the width of the long call spread usually makes this play less expensive to run than a traditional butterfly with calls. The tradeoff is that you're taking on more risk than you would with a traditional butterfly. If the stock continues to rise above strike C, your profit will decline at an accelerated rate and the trade could become a loser fairly quickly. That's because you're short two call spreads, and there's half as much distance between strike C and strike D (short spreads) as there is between strike A and strike C (long spread).

Ideally, you want the options at strike C and D to expire worthless, while retaining maximum value for the long call at strike A.

OPTIONS GUY'S TIPS:

☞ The lower the stock price is below strike price A when you initiate the play, the more bullish this play becomes. The benefit is that it will cost less to establish, which means your maximum potential loss will be lower. However, the stock will need to make a bigger move to hit the sweet spot.

☞ Because of the bullish bias on this play, it may be an affordable alternative to long calls (play one) when calls are prohibitively expensive because of high implied volatility. This is especially the case if you're anticipating a decrease in volatility after a bullish move. Whereas a long call owner wants implied volatility to increase, you'll want to see a decrease in implied volatility after this play is established.

BREAK-EVEN AT EXPIRATION

There are two break-even points for this play:

- Strike A plus the net debit paid
- Strike D minus one-half of the net debit paid

THE SWEET SPOT

You want the stock to be exactly at strike C at expiration.

MAXIMUM POTENTIAL PROFIT

Potential profit is limited to strike C minus strike A minus the net debit paid.

MAXIMUM POTENTIAL LOSS

Risk is limited to the net debit paid.

MARGIN REQUIREMENT

After the trade is paid for, no additional margin is required.

AS TIME GOES BY

For this play, time decay is your friend. Ideally, you want all of the options except the call with strike A to expire worthless.

IMPLIED VOLATILITY

After the play is established, the effect of implied volatility depends on where the stock is relative to your strike prices.

If the stock is at or near strike C, you want volatility to decrease. Your main concern is the three options you sold. A decrease in implied volatility will cause those near-the-money options to decrease in value, thereby increasing the overall value of the butterfly. In addition, you want the stock price to remain stable around strike C, and a decrease in implied volatility suggests that may be the case.

If the stock price is approaching or outside strike A or D, in general you want volatility to increase. An increase in volatility will increase the value of the option you own at the near-the-money strike, while having less effect on the short options at strike C.

CHECK YOUR PLAY WITH TRADEKING TOOLS

- Use TradeKing's *Profit + Loss Calculator* to establish break-even points, evaluate how your strategy might change as expiration approaches, and analyze the Greeks.

- Use the *Technical Analysis Tool* to look for bullish indicators.

CHRISTMAS TREE BUTTERFLY W/ PUTS

THE SETUP

- Buy a put, strike price D
- Skip over strike price C
- Sell three puts, strike price B
- Buy two puts, strike price A
- Generally, the stock will be at or around strike D

NOTE: Strike prices are equidistant, and all options have the same expiration month.

WHO SHOULD RUN IT

Seasoned Veterans and higher

WHEN TO RUN IT

 You're slightly bearish. You want the stock to fall to strike B and then stop.

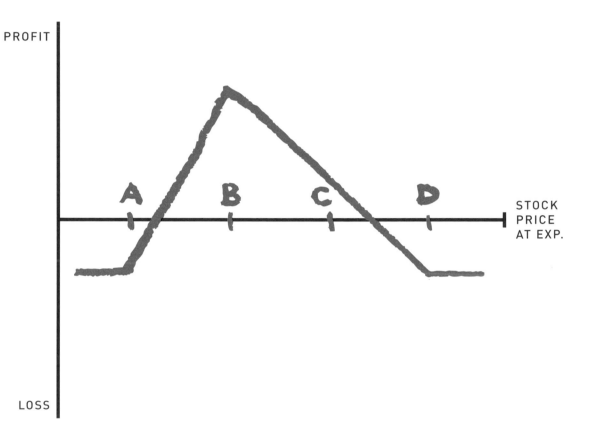

THE STRATEGY

You can think of this play as simultaneously buying one long put spread (play eleven) with strikes D and B and selling two short put spreads (play thirteen) with strikes B and A. Because the long put spread skips over strike C, the distance between its strikes will be twice as wide as the strikes in the short put spread. In other words, if the width from strike D to strike B is 5.00, the width from strike B to strike A will be 2.50.

While a traditional butterfly with puts (play twenty-nine) is often used as a neutral strategy, this play is usually run with a slightly bearish directional bias. To reach the sweet spot, the stock price needs to drop a bit.

Selling two short put spreads with half the width of the long put spread usually makes this play less expensive to run than a traditional butterfly with puts. The tradeoff is that you're taking on more risk than you would with a traditional butterfly. If the stock continues to fall below strike B, your profit will decline at an accelerated rate and the trade could become a loser fairly quickly. That's because you're short two put spreads, and there's half as much distance between strike B and strike A (short spreads) as there is between strike D and strike B (long spread).

Ideally, you want the options at strike A and B to expire worthless, while retaining maximum value for the long put at strike D.

OPTIONS GUY'S TIPS:

☞ The higher the stock price is above strike price D when you initiate the play, the more bearish this play becomes. The benefit is that it will cost less to establish, which means your maximum potential loss will be lower. However, the stock will need to make a bigger move to hit the sweet spot.

☞ Because of the bearish bias on this play, it may be an affordable alternative to a long put (play two) when puts are prohibitively expensive because of high implied volatility. This is especially the case if you're anticipating a decrease in volatility after a bearish move. Whereas a long put owner wants implied volatility to increase, you'll want to see a decrease in implied volatility after this play is established.

BREAK-EVEN AT EXPIRATION

There are two break-even points for this play:

- Strike D minus the net debit paid
- Strike A plus half the net debit paid

THE SWEET SPOT

You want the stock to be exactly at strike B at expiration.

MAXIMUM POTENTIAL PROFIT

Potential profit is limited to strike D minus strike B minus the net debit paid.

MAXIMUM POTENTIAL LOSS

Risk is limited to the net debit paid.

MARGIN REQUIREMENT

After the trade is paid for, no additional margin is required.

AS TIME GOES BY

For this play, time decay is your friend. Ideally, you want all of the options except the put with strike D to expire worthless.

IMPLIED VOLATILITY

After the play is established, the effect of implied volatility depends on where the stock is relative to your strike prices.

If the stock is at or near strike B, you want volatility to decrease. Your main concern is the three options you sold. A decrease in implied volatility will cause those near-the-money options to decrease in value, thereby increasing the overall value of the butterfly. In addition, you want the stock price to remain stable around strike B, and a decrease in implied volatility suggests that may be the case.

If the stock price is approaching or outside strike D or A, in general you want volatility to increase. An increase in volatility will increase the value of the option you own at the near-the-money strike, while having less effect on the short options at strike B.

CHECK YOUR PLAY WITH TRADEKING TOOLS

- Use TradeKing's *Profit + Loss Calculator* to establish break-even points, evaluate how your strategy might change as expiration approaches, and analyze the Greeks.

- Use the *Technical Analysis Tool* to look for bearish indicators.

LONG CONDOR SPREAD W/ CALLS

THE SETUP

- Buy a call, strike price A
- Sell a call, strike price B
- Sell a call, strike price C
- Buy a call, strike price D
- Generally, the stock will be between strike price B and strike price C

NOTE: All options have the same expiration month.

WHO SHOULD RUN IT

Veterans and higher

WHEN TO RUN IT

 You're anticipating minimal movement on the stock within a specific time frame.

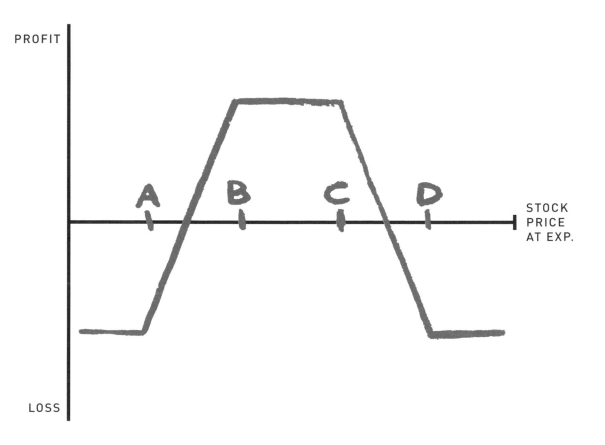

THE STRATEGY

You can think of a long condor spread with calls as simultaneously running an in-the-money long call spread (play ten) and an out-of-the-money short call spread (play twelve). Ideally, you want the short call spread to expire worthless, while the long call spread achieves its maximum value with strikes A and B in-the-money.

Typically, the stock will be halfway between strike B and strike C when you construct your spread. If the stock is not in the center at initiation, the play will be either bullish or bearish.

The distance between strikes A and B is usually the same as the distance between strikes C and D. However, the distance between strikes B and C may vary to give you a wider sweet spot (see Options Guy's Tips).

You want the stock price to end up somewhere between strike B and strike C at expiration. Condor spreads have a wider sweet spot than the butterflies. But (as always) there's a tradeoff. In this case, it's that your potential profit is lower.

🧑 OPTIONS GUY'S TIPS:

☞ You may wish to consider ensuring that strike B and strike C are around one standard deviation away from the stock price at initiation. That will increase your probability of success. However, the further these strike prices are from the current stock price, the lower the potential profit will be from this play.

☞ Some investors may wish to run this play using index options rather than options on individual stocks. That's because historically, indexes have not been as volatile as individual stocks. Fluctuations in an index's component stock prices tend to cancel one another out, lessening the volatility of the index as a whole.

☞ As a general rule of thumb, you may wish to consider running this play approximately 30–45 days from expiration to take advantage of accelerating time decay as expiration approaches. Of course, this depends on the underlying stock and market conditions such as implied volatility.

⓪ BREAK-EVEN AT EXPIRATION

There are two break-even points:

- Strike A plus the net debit paid
- Strike D minus the net debit paid

💲 THE SWEET SPOT

You achieve maximum profit if the stock price is anywhere between strike B and strike C at expiration.

⬆ MAXIMUM POTENTIAL PROFIT

Potential profit is limited to strike B minus strike A minus the net debit paid.

⬇ MAXIMUM POTENTIAL LOSS

Risk is limited to the net debit paid to establish the condor.

% MARGIN REQUIREMENT

After the trade is paid for, no additional margin is required.

🕗 AS TIME GOES BY

For this play, time decay is your friend. Ideally, you want the options with strike C and strike D to expire worthless, and the options with strike A and strike B to retain their intrinsic values.

⊕ IMPLIED VOLATILITY

After the play is established, the effect of implied volatility depends on where the stock is relative to your strike prices.

If the stock is near or between strikes B and C, you want volatility to decrease. Your main concern is the two options you sold at those strikes. A decrease in implied volatility will cause those options to decrease in value, thereby increasing the overall value of the condor. In addition, you want the stock price to remain stable, and a decrease in implied volatility suggests that may be the case.

If the stock price is approaching or outside strike A or D, in general you want volatility to increase. An increase in volatility will increase the value of the option you own at the near-the-money strike, while having less effect on the short options at strikes B and C.

✔ CHECK YOUR PLAY WITH TRADEKING TOOLS

- Use the **Profit + Loss Calculator** to establish break-even points, evaluate how your strategy might change as expiration approaches, and analyze the Greeks.

- Use the **Probability Calculator** to verify that strikes B and strike C are about one standard deviation away from the stock price.

LONG CONDOR SPREAD W/ PUTS

THE SETUP

• Buy a put, strike price A

• Sell a put, strike price B

• Sell a put, strike price C

• Buy a put, strike price D

• Generally, the stock will be between strike price B and strike price C

NOTE: All options have the same expiration month.

WHO SHOULD RUN IT

Veterans and higher

WHEN TO RUN IT

 You're anticipating minimal movement on the stock within a specific time frame.

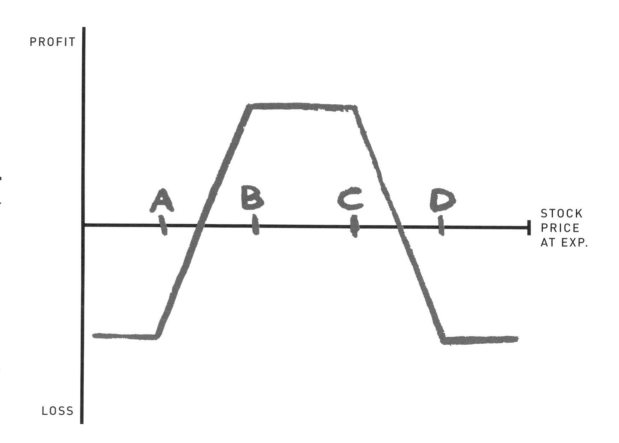

THE STRATEGY

You can think of long condor spread with puts as simultaneously running an in-the-money short put spread (play thirteen) and an out-of-the-money long put spread (play eleven). Ideally, you want the short put spread to expire worthless, while the long put spread achieves its maximum value with strikes C and D in-the-money.

Typically, the stock will be halfway between strike B and strike C when you construct your spread. If the stock is not in the center at initiation, the play will be either bullish or bearish.

The distance between strikes A and B is usually the same as the distance between strikes C and D. However, the distance between strikes B and C may vary to give you a wider sweet spot (see Options Guy's Tips).

You want the stock price to end up somewhere between strike B and strike C at expiration. Condor spreads have a wider sweet spot than the butterflies. But (as always) there's a tradeoff. In this case, it's that your potential profit is lower.

👤 OPTIONS GUY'S TIPS:

☞ You may wish to consider ensuring that strike B and strike C are around one standard deviation away from the stock price at initiation. That will increase your probability of success. However, the further these strike prices are from the current stock price, the lower the potential profit will be from this play.

☞ Some investors may wish to run this play using index options rather than options on individual stocks. That's because historically, indexes have not been as volatile as individual stocks. Fluctuations in an index's component stock prices tend to cancel one another out, lessening the volatility of the index as a whole.

☞ As a general rule of thumb, you may wish to consider running this play approximately 30–45 days from expiration to take advantage of accelerating time decay as expiration approaches. Of course, this depends on the underlying stock and market conditions such as implied volatility.

ⓞ BREAK-EVEN AT EXPIRATION

There are two break-even points:

- Strike A plus the net debit paid
- Strike D minus the net debit paid

💲 THE SWEET SPOT

You achieve maximum profit if the stock price is anywhere between strike B and strike C at expiration.

⬆ MAXIMUM POTENTIAL PROFIT

Potential profit is limited to strike D minus strike C minus the net debit paid.

⬇ MAXIMUM POTENTIAL LOSS

Risk is limited to the net debit paid to establish the condor.

% MARGIN REQUIREMENT

After the trade is paid for, no additional margin is required.

🕐 AS TIME GOES BY

For this play, time decay is your friend. Ideally, you want the options with strike A and strike B to expire worthless, and the options with strike C and strike D to retain their intrinsic values.

⚙ IMPLIED VOLATILITY

After the play is established, the effect of implied volatility depends on where the stock is relative to your strike prices.

If the stock is near or between strikes C and B, you want volatility to decrease. Your main concern is the two options you sold at those strikes. A decrease in implied volatility will cause those options to decrease in value, thereby increasing the overall value of the condor. In addition, you want the stock price to remain stable, and a decrease in implied volatility suggests that may be the case.

If the stock price is approaching or outside strike D or A, in general you want volatility to increase. An increase in volatility will increase the value of the option you own at the near-the-money strike, while having less effect on the short options at strikes C and B.

✓ CHECK YOUR PLAY WITH TRADEKING TOOLS

- Use the **Profit + Loss Calculator** to establish break-even points, evaluate how your strategy might change as expiration approaches, and analyze the Greeks.

- Use the **Probability Calculator** to verify that strikes B and strike C are about one standard deviation away from the stock price.

IRON CONDOR

THE SETUP

- Buy a put, strike price A

- Sell a put, strike price B

- Sell a call, strike price C

- Buy a call, strike price D

- Generally, the stock will be between strike price B and strike price C

NOTE: All options have the same expiration month.

WHO SHOULD RUN IT

Veterans and higher

WHEN TO RUN IT

 You're anticipating minimal movement on the stock within a specific time frame.

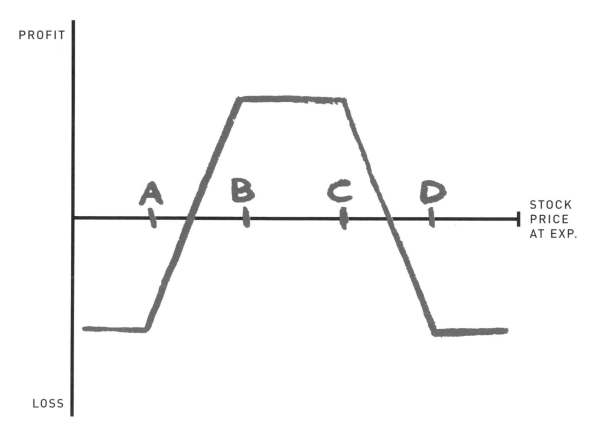

THE STRATEGY

You can think of this play as simultaneously running an out-of-the-money short put spread (play thirteen) and an out-of-the-money short call spread (play twelve). Some investors consider this to be a more attractive strategy than a long condor spread with calls or puts because you receive a net credit into your account right off the bat.

Typically, the stock will be halfway between strike B and strike C when you construct your spread. If the stock is not in the center at initiation, the play will be either bullish or bearish.

The distance between strikes A and B is usually the same as the distance between strikes C and D. However, the distance between strikes B and C may vary to give you a wider sweet spot (see Options Guy's Tip).

You want the stock price to end up somewhere between strike B and strike C at expiration. An iron condor spread has a wider sweet spot than an iron butterfly. But (as always) there's a tradeoff. In this case, your potential profit is lower.

👤 OPTIONS GUY'S TIPS:

☞ One advantage of this strategy is that you want all of the options to expire worthless. If that happens, you won't have to pay any commissions to get out of your position.

☞ You may wish to consider ensuring that strike B and strike C are around one standard deviation or more away from the stock price at initiation. That will increase your probability of success. However, the further these strike prices are from the current stock price, the lower the potential profit will be from this play.

☞ As a general rule of thumb, you may wish to consider running this play approximately 30–45 days from expiration to take advantage of accelerating time decay as expiration approaches. Of course, this depends on the underlying stock and market conditions such as implied volatility.

☞ Some investors may wish to run this play using index options rather than options on individual stocks. That's because historically, indexes have not been as volatile as individual stocks. Fluctuations in an index's component stock prices tend to cancel one another out, lessening the volatility of the index as a whole.

🄌 BREAK-EVEN AT EXPIRATION

There are two break-even points:

- Strike B minus the net credit received
- Strike C plus the net credit received

💲 THE SWEET SPOT

You achieve maximum profit if the stock price is between strike B and strike C at expiration.

⬆ MAXIMUM POTENTIAL PROFIT

Profit is limited to the net credit received.

⬇ MAXIMUM POTENTIAL LOSS

Risk is limited to strike B minus strike A, minus the net credit received.

% MARGIN REQUIREMENT

See Appendix A for margin requirement.

🕐 AS TIME GOES BY

For this play, time decay is your friend. You want all four options to expire worthless.

✦ IMPLIED VOLATILITY

After the play is established, the effect of implied volatility depends on where the stock is relative to your strike prices.

If the stock is near or between strikes B and C, you want volatility to decrease. This will decrease the value of all of the options, and ideally, you'd like the iron condor to expire worthless. In addition, you want the stock price to remain stable, and a decrease in implied volatility suggests that may be the case.

If the stock price is approaching or outside strike A or D, in general you want volatility to increase. An increase in volatility will increase the value of the option you own at the near-the-money strike, while having less effect on the short options at strikes B and C. So the overall value of the iron condor will decrease, making it less expensive to close your position.

✔ CHECK YOUR PLAY WITH TRADEKING TOOLS

- Use the **Profit + Loss Calculator** to establish break-even points, evaluate how your strategy might change as expiration approaches, and analyze the Greeks.

- Use the **Probability Calculator** to verify that strikes B and strike C are about one standard deviation away from the stock price.

DOUBLE DIAGONAL

THE SETUP

• Buy an out-of-the-money put, strike price A
(Approximately 60 days from expiration – "back-month")

• Sell an out-of-the-money put, strike price B
(Approximately 30 days from expiration – "front-month")

• Sell an out-of-the-money call, strike price C
(Approximately 30 days from expiration – "front-month")

• Buy an out-of-the-money call, strike price D
(Approximately 60 days from expiration – "back-month")

• Generally, the stock price will be between strike price B and strike price C

If the stock price is still between strike price B and strike price C at expiration of the front-month options:

• Sell another put at strike price B and sell another call at strike price C, with the same expiration as the options at strike price A and strike price D.

WHO SHOULD RUN IT

All-Stars only

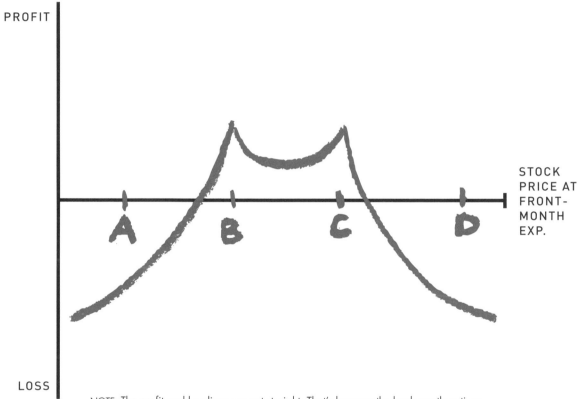

NOTE: The profit and loss lines are not straight. That's because the back-month options are still open when the front-month options expire. Straight lines and hard angles usually indicate that all options in the play have the same expiration date.

WHEN TO RUN IT

 You're anticipating minimal movement on the stock over at least two option expiration cycles.

THE STRATEGY

At the outset of this play, you're simultaneously running a diagonal spread with calls (play twenty-six) and a diagonal spread with puts (play twenty-seven). Both of those strategies are time-decay plays. You're taking advantage of the fact that the time value of the front-month options decay at a more accelerated rate than the back-month options.

At first glance, this seems like an exceptionally complicated option play. But if you think of it as capitalizing on minimal stock movement over multiple option expiration cycles, it's not terribly difficult to understand how it works.

Typically, the stock will be halfway between strike B and strike C when you establish the play. If the stock is not in the center at this point, the play will have a bullish or bearish bias. You want the stock to remain between strike B and strike C, so the options you've sold will expire worthless and you will capture the entire premium. The put you bought at strike A and the call you bought at strike D serve to reduce your risk over the course of the play in case the stock makes a larger-than-expected move in either direction.

You should try to establish this play for a net credit. But you may not be able to do so because the front-month options you're selling have less time value than the back-month options you're buying. So you might choose to run it for a small net debit and make up the cost when you sell the second set of options after front-month expiration.

As expiration of the front-month options approaches, hopefully the stock will be somewhere between strike B and strike C. To complete this play, you'll need to buy to close the front-month options and sell another put at strike B and another call at strike C. These options will have the same expiration as the ones at strike A and strike D. This is known as "rolling" out in time. (If you don't already understand the concept of rolling, see "How We Roll" on P.134.)

Most traders buy to close the front-month options before they expire because they don't want to carry extra risk over the weekend after expiration. This helps guard against unexpected price swings between the close of the market on the expiration date and the open on the following trading day.

Once you've sold the additional options at strike B and strike C and all the options have the same expiration date, you'll discover you've gotten yourself into a good old iron condor (play thirty-nine). The goal at this point is still the same as at the outset—you want the stock price to remain between strike B and C. Ultimately, you want all of the options to expire out-of-the-money and worthless so you can pocket the total credit from running all segments of this play.

Some investors consider this to be a nice alternative to simply running a longer-term iron condor, because you can capture the premium for the short options at strike B and C twice.

OPTIONS GUY'S TIPS:

☞ For this playbook, I'm using the example of a double diagonal with options 30 and 60 days from expiration. However, it is possible to use back-month options with an expiration date that's further out in time. If you're going to use more than a one-month interval between the front-month and the back-month options, you need to understand the ins and outs of "rolling " (See "How We Roll" on P.134.)

☞ Whenever you're short options, you have to be extremely careful during the last week prior to expiration. In other words, if one of the front-month options you've sold is in-the-money during the last week, it will increase in value much more rapidly than the back-month options you bought. (That's why this period is sometimes referred to as "gamma week.") So if it appears that a front-month option will expire in-the-money, you may wish to consider rolling it before you reach the last week prior to expiration. (Once again, see "How We Roll" on P.134. Are you getting the feeling that rolling is a really important concept to understand before you run this play?)

☞ To run this play, you need to know how to manage the risk of early assignment on your short options. So be sure to read, "What Is Early Exercise and Assignment and Why Does It Happen?" on P.140.

☞ Some investors may wish to run this play using index options rather than options on individual stocks. That's because historically, indexes have not been as volatile as individual stocks. Fluctuations in an index's component stock prices tend to cancel one another out, lessening the volatility of the index as a whole.

⓿ BREAK-EVEN AT EXPIRATION

It is possible to approximate your break-even points, but there are too many variables to give an exact formula.

Because there are multiple expiration dates for the options in this play, a pricing model must be used to "guesstimate" what the value of the back-month options will be when the front-month options expire. TradeKing's *Profit + Loss Calculator* can help in this regard. But keep in mind, the *Profit + Loss Calculator* assumes that all other variables such as implied volatility, interest rates, etc. remain constant over the life of the trade, and they may not behave that way in reality.

$ THE SWEET SPOT

The sweet spot is not as straightforward as it is with most other plays. You might benefit a little more if the stock winds up at or around strike B or strike C at the front-month expiration because you'll be selling an option that's closer to being at-the-money. That will jack up the overall time value you receive.

However, the closer the stock price is to strike B or C, the more you might lose sleep because there is increased risk of the play becoming a loser if it continues to make a bullish or bearish move beyond the short strike. So running this strategy is a lot easier to manage if the stock stays right between strike B and strike C for the duration of the play.

⬆ MAXIMUM POTENTIAL PROFIT

Potential profit for this play is limited to the net credit received for the sale of the front-month options at strike B and strike C, plus the net credit received for the sale of the second round of options at strike B and strike C, minus the net debit paid for the back-month options at strike A and strike D.

NOTE: Because you don't know exactly how much you'll receive from the sale of the additional options at strikes B and C, you can only "guesstimate" your potential profit when establishing this play.

⬇ MAXIMUM POTENTIAL LOSS

If established for a net credit, at initiation of the play risk is limited to strike B minus strike A minus the net credit received. If you are able to sell an additional set of options at strikes B and C, deduct this additional premium from the total risk.

If established for a net debit, at initiation of the play risk is limited to strike B minus strike A plus the debit paid. If you are able to sell an additional set of options at strikes B and C, deduct this additional premium from the total risk.

NOTE: You can't precisely calculate your risk at initiation of this play, because it depends on the premium received (if any) for the sale of the additional options at strikes B and C.

% MARGIN REQUIREMENT

See Appendix A for margin requirement.

☻ AS TIME GOES BY

For this play, time decay is your friend. Ideally, you want all of the options to expire worthless.

⟳ IMPLIED VOLATILITY

After the play is established, although you don't want the stock price to move much, it's desirable for volatility to increase around the time the front-month options expire. That way, you will receive more premium for the sale of the additional options at strike B and strike C.

After front-month expiration, the effect of implied volatility depends on where the stock is relative to your strike prices.

If the stock is near or between strikes B and C, you want volatility to decrease. This will decrease the value of all of the options, and ideally, you'd like everything to expire worthless. In addition, you want the stock price to remain stable, and a decrease in implied volatility suggests that may be the case.

If the stock price is approaching or outside strike A or D, in general you want volatility to increase. An increase in volatility will increase the value of the option you own at the near-the-money strike, while having less effect on the short options at strikes B and C.

✓ CHECK YOUR PLAY WITH TRADEKING TOOLS

• Use TradeKing's *Profit + Loss Calculator* to establish break-even points, evaluate how your strategy might change as expiration approaches, and analyze the Greeks.

FINAL THOUGHTS

THE PLAYERS IN THE GAME

Many option traders don't understand who might be buying or selling the options on the other end of their transaction. Fortunately, after reading this section, you won't be one of them.

Buying or selling an option is a process quite similar to buying or selling stock. It's not some mystical process just because it's a different type of security. In fact, it trades pretty much like any other security.

In the option market, you're dealing with four different entities: retail investors like you, institutional traders, broker-dealers and "market makers." The generic term "trader" is often used interchangeably for any of these players.

Orders generated by each player are routed to entities called "exchanges." You probably already know how exchanges work. But figuring out just how options change hands can be a little confusing. So let's take a look at just who each player is, then we'll look at how your option orders get executed.

RETAIL INVESTORS are individuals like you who are buying and selling options with their own money for personal profit. Their objective is usually to make a significant percentage gain on their initial investments. Normally, individual retail investors will be trading on a smaller scale than the other players in the game.

INSTITUTIONAL TRADERS are professionals trading for large entities like mutual funds, hedge funds, etc. Oftentimes they will trade options to hedge their positions, but they may also trade options as pure speculation.

BROKER-DEALERS are in the game to facilitate trades. These are firms like TradeKing, that accept orders on behalf of clients and then ensure they are executed in the open market at the best available price. This is done in exchange for commissions on the trade. In addition to facilitating trades, a dealer may also choose to buy or sell options for its own benefit, whereas a regular broker won't. So the combined term "broker-dealer" encompasses all of the players that serve these particular functions.

MARKET MAKERS are the 800 lb. gorilla in the game. They're obligated to make bids and offers on the options traded on specific securities. Thus, market makers provide liquidity in the options marketplace.

In other words, market makers stand ready to take the opposite side of a trade if and when one of the other players wants to buy or sell an option. Market makers provide a firm bid and ask (offer) price in order to facilitate trading on that option.

In theory, market makers earn their profits from the difference between the bid and ask price of options. They try to continually buy at the bid price and sell at a higher ask price, so they'll make a few nickels or dimes on each transaction. And when you're making as many trades as a market maker, that loose change can really add up. In practice, the picture is a little more complex. But for now, the above scenario is all you really need to know.

EXCHANGES exist to maintain a fair and orderly marketplace and to provide timely dissemination of price information. Any time you place an option order, it is routed to an exchange, where buyers are matched with sellers. Exchanges can be either a physical "open outcry" location where traders meet to conduct transactions or an electronic platform.

SO WHO'S ON THE OTHER SIDE OF MY OPTION TRADE?

When you enter an option order with TradeKing, we look in the marketplace for the national best bid or offer price for your trade. Your transaction is then matched with the entity providing that bid or offer.

Much of the time you will be trading with a market maker. However, you may instead wind up trading with an institutional trader, a dealer, or another retail client. It really makes no difference who you're trading with, as long as your order is executed at a favorable price.

Ultimately, what this all means is that there will always be a market for any exchange-traded option you would like to buy or sell. You may not always like the market for a given option, but rest assured it will always be there for you to participate in should you choose to do so.

Where Your Option Orders Go

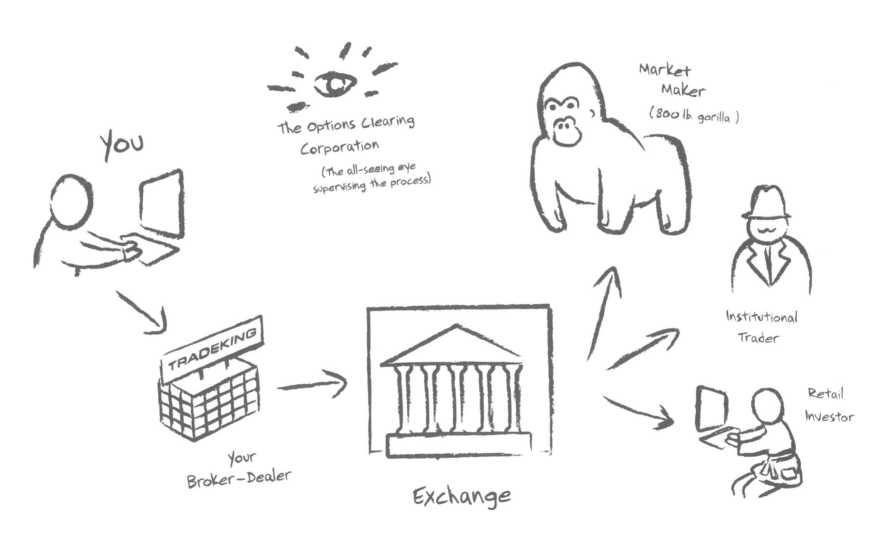

You

The Options Clearing Corporation

(The all-seeing eye supervising the process)

Your Broker-Dealer

Exchange

Market Maker
(800 lb. gorilla)

Institutional Trader

Retail Investor

HOW WE ROLL

AN INTRODUCTION TO THE CONCEPT OF "ROLLING"

Rolling is one of the most common ways to adjust an option position. It's possible to roll either a long or short option position, but in this section, I'm going to focus on the short side.

When you decide to roll, you've changed your outlook on the underlying stock and fear that your short options are going to be assigned. The objective is to put off assignment, or even avoid it altogether. It's an advanced technique, and it's one you need to thoroughly understand before executing.

When you roll a short position, you're buying to close an existing position and selling to open a new one. You're tweaking the strike prices on your options, and / or "rolling" the expiration further out in time. But rolling is never guaranteed to work. In fact, you might end up compounding your losses. So exercise caution and don't get greedy.

To help you grasp the concept of rolling, I'll examine the process of rolling three basic

positions: a covered call, a cash-secured put, and a short call spread. This section is meant to be an introduction to how rolling works, so the examples I present are somewhat simplified.

You might also notice I use some lingo in this section that I didn't use very much throughout the rest of the book. It's safe to assume if you don't thoroughly understand the terminology, you should learn more about options before attempting this maneuver.

ROLLING A COVERED CALL

Imagine you're running a 30-day covered call (play six) on stock XYZ with a strike price of $90. That means you own 100 shares of XYZ stock, and you've sold one 90-strike call a month from expiration. When you sold the call, the stock price was $87.50, and you received a premium of $1.30, or $130 total, since one contract equals 100 shares. Now, with expiration fast approaching, the stock has gone up to $92. In all probability you will be assigned and have to sell the stock at $90.

The only way to avoid assignment for sure is to buy back the 90-strike call before it is assigned, and cancel your obligation. However, the 90-strike call is now trading for $2.10, so it will hurt a bit to buy it back. To help offset the cost of buying back the call, you're going to "roll up and out."

That means you want to go "up" in strike price and "out" in time. The idea is to balance the decrease in premium for selling a higher OTM strike price versus the greater premium you'll receive for selling an option that is further from expiration (and thus has more "time value").

Here's an example of how that might work.

Using TradeKing's spread order screen, you enter a buy-to-close order for the front-month 90-strike call. In the same trade, you sell to open an OTM 95-strike call (rolling up) that's 60 days from expiration (rolling out). Due to higher time value, the back-month 95-strike call will be trading for $2.30. Since you're paying $2.10 to buy back the front-month call and receiving $2.30 for the back-month call, this trade can be accomplished for a net credit of $0.20 ($2.30 sale price - $2.10 purchase price) or $20 total.

Let's look at all the good news and bad news surrounding this trade. As you'll see, it's a double-edged sword.

Since you've raised the strike price to $95, you have more profit potential on the stock. The obligation to sell was at $90, but now it's at $95. The bad news is, you had to buy back the front-month call for 80 cents more than you received when selling it ($2.10 paid to close - $1.30 received to open). On the other hand, you've more than covered the cost of buying it back by selling the back-month 95-strike call for more premium. So that's good.

But you have to consider the fact that there are still 60 days before the new options expire, and you don't really know what will happen with the stock during that time. You'll just have to keep your fingers crossed and hope for the best.

If the back-month 95-strike short call expires worthless when all's said and done in 60 days, you wind up with a $1.50 net credit. Here's the math: You lost a total of $0.80 after buying back the 90-strike front-month call. However, you received a premium of $2.30 for the 95-strike call, so you netted $1.50 ($2.30 back-month premium - $0.80 front-month loss) or $150 total. That's not a bad outcome (see Ex.1).

However, if the market makes a big move upward in the next 60 days, you might be tempted to roll up and out again. But beware.

You want to avoid assignment →

EX. 1: ROLLING A CALL UP AND OUT

Here comes the roll {

Existing Position: 30-day 90-strike call Premium received	+$1.30
Premium paid to close 90-strike call	-$2.10
Premium received to open 60-day 95-strike call	+$2.30
Net credit from the roll	+$0.20

$1.30 initial premium + $0.20 net credit from roll = **+$1.50 net total** from this series of trades. (TradeKing commissions would be $11.20.)

You want to avoid assignment →

EX. 2: ROLLING A PUT DOWN AND OUT

Here comes the roll {

Existing Position: 30-day 50-strike put Premium received	+$0.90
Premium paid to close 50-strike put	-$1.55
Premium received to open 90-day 47.50-strike put	+$1.70
Net credit from the roll	+$0.15

$0.90 initial premium + $0.15 net credit from roll = **+$1.05 net total** from this series of trades. (TradeKing commissions would be $11.20.)

Every time you roll up and out, you may be taking a loss on the front-month call. Furthermore, you still have not secured any gains on the back-month call or on the stock appreciation, because the market still has time to move against you. And that means you could wind up compounding your losses. So come to think of it, rolling's not really a double-edged sword. It's more like a quadruple-edged shaving razor.

ROLLING A CASH-SECURED PUT

To avoid assignment on a short put, the roll here is "down and out."

For example, let's say you've sold a 30-day cash-secured put (play five) on stock XYZ with a strike price of $50. And let's say you received $0.90 for the put when the stock was trading at $51. Now, close to expiration, the stock has dropped and it's trading at $48.50.

The only way to avoid assignment for sure is to buy back the front-month 50-strike put before it is assigned, and cancel your obligation. The problem is, the front-month put you originally sold for $0.90 is now trading at $1.55. Here's how you roll.

Using TradeKing's spread order screen, you enter a buy-to-close order for the front-month 50-strike put. In the same trade, you sell to open a back-month 47.50-strike put (rolling down), 90 days from expiration (rolling out) which is trading for $1.70. By doing this, you'll receive a net credit of $0.15 ($1.70 back-month sale price - $1.55 front-month purchase price) or $15 total.

You were able to roll for a net credit even though the back-month put is further OTM because of

the considerable increase in time value of the 90-day option.

If the 47.50-strike put expires worthless, when all is said and done in 90 days, you'll net $1.05. Here's the math: You lost a total of $0.65 on the front-month put ($1.55 paid to close - $0.90 received to open). However, you received a premium of $1.70 for the 47.50-strike put, so you netted $1.05 ($1.70 back-month premium - $0.65 front-month loss) or $105 total (see Ex.2).

However, every time you roll down and out, you may be taking a loss on the front-month put. Furthermore, you have not secured any gains on the back-month put because the market still has time to move against you. And that means you could wind up compounding your losses.

👤 OPTIONS GUY'S TIPS:

☞ You should usually roll out the shortest possible time period. That way, you will be faced with less market uncertainty. You may even wish to consider paying a small net debit for the roll to obtain the shorter time period.

☞ As an option you've sold gets in-the-money, you'll have to quickly decide whether or not you're going to roll. As a general rule of thumb, you should consider rolling before options you've sold reach anywhere from 2–4% ITM, depending on the value of the stock and market conditions (e.g., implied volatility). If the option gets too deep ITM, it will be tough to roll for an acceptable net debit, never mind receiving a net credit.

☞ You may want to consider a "pre-emptive roll." That is, you can roll before the option gets ITM if you think it's headed that way. This might lower the cost of buying back the front-month option, and could result in a larger net credit for the roll.

ROLLING A SHORT SPREAD

Rolling a spread works much the same way as rolling an individual option. You will most likely be moving out in time and moving the strike prices either up or down. The difference is you will be trading four different options in one trade instead of two. In other words, you're closing two existing options and opening two new ones.

Now imagine you're bearish on stock XYZ, and it's trading at $53. You might decide to sell a 55/60 short call spread 30 days from expiration, and receive a credit of $1. (You can see how we arrived at the $1 credit in Ex.3, and from this point forward, we'll just focus on the net credit or debit to trade a spread.)

But what if your forecast was wrong, the stock makes a bullish short-term move to $55.50 with 15 days remaining until expiration, and the net cost to buy the spread back is now $1.80? If you're still convinced your forecast is correct and the stock price won't continue to rise, you can roll the spread's strikes up in price and roll expiration out in time.

To do so, you would pay the $1.80 to buy back the 55/60 short call spread and simultaneously sell another short call spread with a short strike of 60, a long strike of 65 and 45 days until expiration. For the 45-day 60/65 strike short call spread you receive a credit of $1.10.

Now instead of being down $0.80 on the trade, if the stock is below $60 at the new expiration date, you'll be up a total of $0.30 ($1.00 net credit to open the 55/60 spread - $1.80 net debit to close the 55/60 spread + $1.10 net credit to open the 60/65 spread = $0.30).

At this point, you really have to hope your forecast is correct and the stock stays below $60. You'll only be up $0.30 on the trade – and that's if everything works out as planned. So if the stock continues to make a bullish move beyond the 60 short strike, things could go south in a hurry.

I can't emphasize enough that when you roll any option, you may be setting yourself up to compound your losses. There's no shame in ditching your position instead of rolling if you're not extremely confident your forecast is correct.

EX. 3: SELLING A SHORT CALL SPREAD

XYZ @ $53
Initial short spread:

Short 55-strike call 30 days from expiration	+$1.25
Long 60-strike call 30 days from expiration	-$0.25
Net credit from initial spread	+$1.00

(TradeKing commissions would be $11.20.)

EX. 4: ROLLING A SHORT CALL SPREAD UP AND OUT

Existing position: 55/60 short call spread 30 days from expiration. Premium received	+$1.00
Debit paid to buy back 55/60 short call spread 15 days from expiration	-$1.80
Credit received for selling 60/65 short call spread 45 days from expiration	+$1.10
Net debit from the roll	-$0.70

$1.00 initial premium received - $1.80 to buy back 55/60 spread + $1.10 net credit for selling 60/65 spread = **+$0.30 net total** from this series of trades. (TradeKing commissions would be $22.40.)

You want to dodge a bullet on this spread ←

Here comes the roll

🧑 OPTIONS GUY'S TIPS:

☞ The concepts addressed in this section apply to any type of two-legged trade, not just short spreads. You can also roll straddles, combinations, front spreads and back spreads. You can even roll one-half of four-legged trades that consist of two spreads, like iron condors (play thirty-nine) and double diagonals (play forty).

☞ Rolling spreads is something iron condor and double diagonal traders absolutely must understand, since both plays consist of two short spreads (one with calls and one with puts).

☞ When you roll a spread, make sure you pull it off all in one trade to help protect against stock movement between the time you close one spread and open another.

KEEPING AN EYE ON POSITION DELTA

I've already explained how delta affects the value of individual options (see "Meet the Greeks" on P.18). Now let's have a look at how you can take delta to the next level. "Position delta" enables you to keep track of the net delta effect on an entire gaggle of options that are based on the same underlying stock.

Think of position delta this way: options act as a substitute for a certain number of shares of the underlying stock. For any stock, you can add up the deltas of all the options in your position and figure out how many shares that position is acting like. That way, you'll always know off the top of your head how it should react when the stock makes a one-point move in either direction.

HOW OPTIONS ACT AS A SUBSTITUTE FOR SHARES OF STOCK

A single call contract with a delta of .01 is a substitute for one share of stock. Here's why.

If the stock price goes up $1, the call should go up by one penny. But generally speaking, an option contract will represent 100 shares of stock. So you need to multiply the delta by 100 shares: $.01 x 100 = $1.

That means if the price of the stock increases $1, the value of your call position should also increase $1. So in essence, it's behaving like one share of stock.

Owning a single call contract with a delta of .50 is similar to owning 50 shares. When the underlying stock goes up $1, the value of the option should increase by $.50. So the value of the overall position will increase by $50. ($.50 x 100 share multiplier = $50.)

It works the same way with puts, but keep in mind that puts have a negative delta. So if you own a put contract with a delta of -.50, it would act like a short position of 50 shares. If the underlying stock goes down $1, the value of the option position should go up $50.

CALCULATING POSITION DELTA FOR A SINGLE-LEG STRATEGY WITH MULTIPLE CONTRACTS

Here's an example. Say you own 10 contracts of XYZ calls, each with a delta of .75. To calculate position delta, multiply .75 x 100 (assuming each contract represents 100 shares) x 10 contracts. This gives you a result of 750.

That means your call options are acting as a substitute for 750 shares of the underlying stock. So you can figure if the stock goes up $1, the position will increase roughly $750. If the underlying stock goes down $1, the position will decrease roughly $750.

EXAMPLE 1:

Long 10 XYZ Calls

Delta = **.75**

Position Delta = **.75 x 100 x 10 = 750**

CALCULATING POSITION DELTA FOR MULTIPLE LEGS AND MULTIPLE STRATEGIES

Much of the time your option plays will be more complex than a few call options with the same strike price. You might use multi-leg strategies, and you might even run different strategies on the same underlying stock at the same time.

Each of those strategies might involve options with different strike prices and expiration dates. For example, you might wind up running an iron condor (play thirty-nine) and a long calendar spread with calls (play twenty-four) simultaneously on the same underlying stock.

The deltas of some individual options in the complete option position will be positive and some will be negative. But even if the strategies you're running are complex, one glance at position delta can give you a feel for how the value of the position should change if the stock moves one point in either direction.

I don't want to clutter up this section by doing the math across six or seven different legs among several strategies. So let's look at an easy example of how you calculate position delta for a simple multi-leg strategy. For instance, consider a long call spread (play ten) with two legs.

Example 2 shows the details of an XYZ long call spread with a long 55-strike and a short 60-strike, both with the same expiration date. Imagine that with the stock trading at $56.55, we bought 15 contracts of 55-strike calls with a delta of .61 and we sold 15 contracts of 60-strike calls with a delta of .29.

CALCULATING LEG 1

The delta of the 55-strike call is .61. So to determine the total delta, we multiply .61 x 100 share multiplier x 15 contracts. That equals 915.

CALCULATING LEG 2

The delta of the 60-strike call is .29. However, since you're selling the calls, for this part of your position the delta will actually be negative: -0.29.

So the short 60 calls' total delta is -.29 x 100 share multiplier x 15 contracts. That equals -435.

CALCULATING TOTAL POSITION DELTA

Now you simply add the deltas from each leg together to determine your position delta: 915 + (-435) = 480. So the theoretical change in position value based on a $1 move in the underlying stock is $480. Therefore, the total value of this position will behave like 480 shares of stock XYZ.

HOW POSITION DELTA HELPS YOU TO MANAGE YOUR RISK

Your net position delta for options on any underlying stock represents your current risk relative to a change in the stock price. In the long call spread example, you'd need to ask yourself if you're comfortable with having the same risk as being long 480 shares of XYZ stock. If not,

EXAMPLE 2:

Long 15 55-Strike Calls

Delta = **.61**

Position Delta = **.61 x 100 x 15 = 915**

Short 15 60-Strike Calls

Delta = **-.29**

Position Delta = **-.29 x 100 x 15 = -435**

Total Position Delta = **915 + (-435) = 480**

you may want to attend to that risk. You can do so by closing out part of your position or by adding negative deltas, perhaps by buying puts or selling stock short.

The same logic applies if you hold a position with a high negative delta. You will have the same risk as a short position in the stock. To adjust your risk, you could dump part of your position, buy calls, or buy the stock.

DON'T FORGET ABOUT GAMMA

Just as gamma will affect the delta of one option as the stock price changes, it will affect the net delta of your entire position as well. So it's important to keep in mind that your position delta will change with every little movement in the stock. And gamma's effect on position delta can be huge, because we're talking about multiple option contracts.

The number of shares for which your options act as a substitute will change every time the stock price changes. That's why it's a good idea to keep an eye on your position delta throughout the life of your option position.

If you have a TradeKing account, keeping an eye on position delta is easy. Just look at the "Option View" in your "Holdings" page, or use the *Profit + Loss Calculator*, and we'll do the math for you.

WHAT IS EARLY EXERCISE AND ASSIGNMENT AND WHY DOES IT HAPPEN?

Early exercise happens when the owner of a call or put invokes his or her contractual rights before expiration. As a result, an option seller will be assigned, shares of stock will change hands, and the result is not always pretty for the seller. (It's important to note that when I talk about early exercise and assignment I'm referring only to "American-style" stock options.)

Being required to buy or sell shares of stock before you originally expected to do so can impact the potential risk or reward of your overall position and become a major headache. But chances are, if you sell options – either as a simple position or as part of a more complex play – sooner or later, you'll get hit with a surprise early assignment. Many traders fail to plan for this possibility and feel like their strategy is falling apart when it does happen.

The strategies that can be messed up the most by early assignment tend to be multi-leg strategies like long and short spreads, butterflies, long calendar spreads and diagonal spreads. The latter two strategies can go particularly haywire as a result of early assignment, because you're dealing with multiple expiration dates.

In most cases, it's a bad idea for option owners to exercise early. However, there are a few instances when exercising early does make sense.

As an option seller, you're at risk of early assignment at any time. And it's impossible to predict whether an option owner will exercise early for the right reasons or the wrong reasons. But understanding the pros and cons of early exercise can make you more aware of when you might be at risk of early assignment.

The likelihood of a short option being assigned early depends on whether the option you sold is a call or a put. So let's examine each separately.

THREE REASONS NOT TO EXERCISE CALLS EARLY

KEEP YOUR RISK LIMITED

If you own a call, your risk is limited to the amount you paid for the option, even if the stock drops to zero. But if you own 100 shares of the stock and it completely tanks, you'll be left holding the bag.

If your call is in-the-money prior to expiration, it makes little sense to exercise early. That's because you can be party to gains without assuming the bigger downside that comes with owning the stock. If you do exercise your in-the-money call early and buy the stock, but then the stock falls below your strike price before expiration, you'll really have egg on your face. In this case, you could have let the option expire worthless and bought the stock at a lower price on the open market.

SAVE YOUR CASH

If you exercise a call early and buy the stock, you'll spend cash sooner instead of later. You already know how much you are going to pay for the stock, namely, the call's strike price. So why not keep your cash in an interest-bearing account for as long as possible before you pay for those shares? Disciplined investors look for every opportunity to achieve maximum return on their assets, and this one happens to be a complete no-brainer.

DON'T MISS OUT ON TIME VALUE

By exercising a call early, you may be leaving money on the table in the form of time value left in the option's price. If there is any time value, the call will be trading for more than the amount it is in-the-money. So if you want to own the stock immediately, you could simply sell the call and then apply the proceeds to the purchase of the shares. Factoring in the extra time value, the overall cost you'll pay for the stock will be less than if you had exercised your call outright.

ONE CIRCUMSTANCE WHEN IT MIGHT MAKE SENSE TO EXERCISE A CALL EARLY: APPROACHING DIVIDENDS

The exception to these three rules occurs when a dividend is going to be paid on the stock. Call buyers are not entitled to dividend payments, so if you want to receive the dividend, you have to exercise the in-the-money call and become a stock owner.

If the upcoming dividend amount is larger than the time value remaining in the call's price, it might make sense to exercise the option. But you have to do so prior to the ex-dividend date.

So always be aware of dividends whenever you've sold a call contract – especially when the ex-dividend date occurs close to expiration, the call is in-the-money, and the dividend is relatively large.

PUTS ARE AT GREATER RISK OF EARLY ASSIGNMENT AS TIME VALUE BECOMES NEGLIGIBLE

In the case of puts, the game changes. When you exercise a put, you're selling stock and receiving cash. So it can be tempting to get cash now as opposed to getting cash later. However, once again you must factor time value into the equation.

If you own a put and you want to sell the stock before expiration, it's usually a good idea to sell the put first and then immediately sell the stock. That way, you'll capture the time value for the put along with the value of the stock.

However, as expiration approaches and time value becomes negligible, it's less of a deterrent against early exercise. That's because by exercising you can accomplish your aim all in one simple transaction without any further hassles.

If you've sold a put, remember that the less time value there is in the price of the option as expiration approaches, the more you will be at risk of early assignment. So keep a close eye on the time value left in your short puts and have a plan in place in case you're assigned early.

DIVIDENDS AS A DETERRENT AGAINST EARLY PUT EXERCISE

As opposed to calls, an approaching ex-dividend date can be a deterrent against early exercise for puts. By exercising the put, the owner will receive cash now. However, this will create a short sale of stock if the put owner wasn't long that stock to begin with. So exercising a put option the day before an ex-dividend date means the put owner will have to pay the dividend.

So if you've sold a put, this means you may have a lower chance of being assigned early, but only until the ex-dividend date has passed.

WHAT TO DO IF YOU'RE ASSIGNED EARLY ON A SHORT OPTION IN A MULTI-LEG STRATEGY

Early assignment on a short option in a multi-leg strategy can really pull a leg out from under your play. If this happens, there's no hard-and-fast rule on what to do. Sometimes you'll want to exercise any long options and sometimes you'll just want to close your entire position. But it's always a good idea to keep a swear jar and some small bills near your computer just in case.

If you are assigned early on a multi-leg strategy, feel free to give us a call at TradeKing and we'll try to help you handle it in the most opportune way.

AMERICAN-STYLE VS. EUROPEAN-STYLE OPTIONS

When it comes to exercise and assignment, there are two "styles" of options: European-style and American-style. But don't let the names throw you. They have nothing to do with where the options are traded. In fact, both American- and European-style options are traded on U.S. exchanges. The different styles simply refer to when the options may be exercised and assigned.

AMERICAN-STYLE OPTIONS

can be exercised by the owner at any time before expiration. Thus, the seller of an American-style option may be assigned at any time before expiration.

As of this writing, all equity options are American-style contracts. And generally speaking, options based on exchange-traded funds (ETFs) are also American-style contracts.

EUROPEAN-STYLE OPTIONS

can be exercised only at expiration, so the seller doesn't have to worry about being assigned until then. Most index options are European-style.

Before you set up a position, it's critical to know whether the options you're trading are American- or European-style, so you'll know if early exercise or assignment is a possibility for you.

Just keep in mind that either style of option can still be bought or sold to close your position in the marketplace at any point during the contract's lifetime.

FIVE MISTAKES TO AVOID WHEN TRADING OPTIONS

(ESPECIALLY SINCE AFTER READING THIS SECTION, YOU'LL HAVE NO EXCUSE FOR MAKING THEM)

In nearly 20 years in the securities industry, I've seen option traders of every level make the same mistakes over and over and over again. And the sad part is, most of these mistakes could have been easily avoided.

Throughout this playbook, I've mentioned many pitfalls to watch out for when trading options. Here are five more common mistakes you need to avoid. After all, trading options isn't easy. So why make it harder than it needs to be?

MISTAKE 1: NOT HAVING A DEFINED EXIT PLAN

You've probably heard this one a million times before. When trading options, just as when you're trading stocks, it's critical to control your emotions. That doesn't necessarily mean you need to have ice flowing through your veins, or that you need to swallow your every fear in a superhuman way.

It's much simpler than that: Always have a plan to work, and always work your plan. And no matter what your emotions are telling you to do, don't deviate from it.

HOW YOU CAN TRADE SMARTER

Planning your exit isn't just about minimizing loss on the downside if things go wrong. You should have an exit plan, period – even when a trade is going your way. You need to choose your upside exit point and downside exit point in advance.

But it's important to keep in mind, with options you need more than upside and downside price targets. You also need to plan the time frame for each exit.

Remember: Options are a decaying asset. And that rate of decay accelerates as your expiration date approaches. So if you're long a call or put and the move you predicted doesn't happen within the time period expected, get out and move on to the next trade.

Time decay doesn't always have to hurt you, of course. When you sell options without owning them, you're putting time decay to work for you. In other words, you're successful if time decay erodes the option's price, and you get to keep the premium received for the sale. But keep in mind this premium is your maximum profit if you're short a call or put. The flipside is that you are exposed to potentially substantial risk if the trade goes awry.

The bottom line is: You must have a plan to get out of any trade no matter what kind of play you're running, or whether it's a winner or a loser. I have seen way too many traders not get out soon enough on profitable trades because they got greedy, or stay way too long in losers because they're hoping the trade will move back in their favor.

WHAT IF YOU GET OUT TOO EARLY AND LEAVE SOME UPSIDE ON THE TABLE?

This is the classic trader's worry, and it's often used as a rationale for not sticking with an original plan. Here's the best counterargument I can think of: What if you profit more consistently, reduce your incidence of losses, and sleep better at night?

Trading with a plan helps you establish more successful patterns of trading and keeps your worries more in check. Sure, trading can be exciting, but it's not about one-hit wonders. And it shouldn't be about getting ulcers from worry, either. So make your plan in advance, and then stick to it like super glue.

MISTAKE 2: TRYING TO MAKE UP FOR PAST LOSSES BY "DOUBLING UP"

I've heard many option traders say they would never do something. For example: "I'd never buy really out-of-the-money options," or "I'd never sell in-the-money options." But it's funny how these absolutes seem pretty obvious – until you find yourself in a trade that's moved against you.

Believe me, I've been there. Facing a scenario where a trade does precisely the opposite of what you expect, you're often tempted to break all kinds of personal rules and simply keep on trading the same option you started with. In such cases, traders are often thinking, "Wouldn't it be nice if the entire market was wrong, not me?"

As a stock trader, you've probably heard a justification for "doubling up to catch up": if you liked the stock at 80 when you first bought it, you've got to love it at 50. So it can be tempting to buy more shares and lower the net cost basis on the trade. Be wary, though: What can sometimes make sense for stocks oftentimes does not fly in the options world.

HOW YOU CAN TRADE SMARTER

"Doubling up" on an options strategy almost never works. Options are derivatives, which means their prices don't move the same way or even have the same properties as the underlying stock.

Although doubling up can lower your per-contract cost basis for the entire position, it usually just compounds your risk. So when a trade goes south and you're contemplating the previously unthinkable, just step back and ask yourself: "If I didn't already have a position in place, is this a trade I would make?" If the answer is no, then don't do it.

Close the trade, cut your losses, and find a different opportunity that makes sense now. Options offer great possibilities for leverage using relatively low capital, but they can blow up quickly if you keep digging yourself deeper. It's a much wiser move to accept a loss now instead of setting yourself up for a bigger catastrophe later.

MISTAKE 3: TRADING ILLIQUID OPTIONS

When you get a quote for any option in the marketplace, you'll notice a difference between the bid price (how much someone is willing to pay for an option) and the ask price (how much someone is willing to sell an option for).

Oftentimes, the bid price and the ask price do not reflect what the option is really worth. The "real" value of the option will actually be somewhere near the middle of the bid and ask. And just how far the bid and ask prices deviate from the real value of the option depends on the option's liquidity.

"Liquidity" in the market means there are active buyers and sellers at all times, with heavy competition to fill transactions. This activity drives the bid and ask prices of stocks and options closer together.

The market for stocks is generally more liquid than their related options markets. That's because stock traders are all trading just one stock, whereas people trading options on a given stock have a plethora of contracts to choose from, with different strike prices and different expiration dates.

At-the-money and near-the-money options with near-term expiration are usually the most liquid. So the spread between the bid and ask prices should be narrower than other options traded on the same stock. As your strike price gets further away from the at-the-money strike and / or the expiration date gets further into the future, options will usually be less and less liquid. Consequently, the spread between the bid and ask prices will usually be wider.

Illiquidity in the options market becomes an even more serious issue when you're dealing with illiquid stocks. After all, if the stock is inactive, the options will probably be even more inactive, and the bid / ask spread will be even wider.

Imagine you're about to trade an illiquid option that has a bid price of $2.00 and an ask price of $2.25. That 25-cent difference might not seem like a lot of money to you. In fact, you might not even bend over to pick up a quarter if you saw one in the street. But for a $2.00 option position, 25 cents is a full 12.5% of the price!

Imagine sacrificing 12.5% of any other investment right off the bat. Not too appealing, is it?

HOW YOU CAN TRADE SMARTER

First of all, it makes sense to trade options on stocks with high liquidity in the market. A stock that trades fewer than 1,000,000 shares a day is usually considered illiquid. So options traded on that stock will most likely be illiquid too.

When you're trading, you might want to start by looking at options with open interest of at least 50 times the number of contacts you want to trade. For example, if you're trading 10 contracts, your minimum acceptable liquidity should be 10 x 50, or an open interest of at least 500 contracts.

Obviously, the greater the volume on an option contract, the closer the bid / ask spread is likely to be. Remember to do the math and make sure the width of the spread isn't eating up too much of your initial investment. Because while the numbers may seem insignificant at first, in the long run they can really add up.

Instead of trading illiquid options on companies like Joe's Tree Cutting Service, you might as well trade the stock instead. There are plenty of liquid stocks out there with opportunities to trade options on them.

MISTAKE 4: WAITING TOO LONG TO BUY BACK SHORT STRATEGIES

I can boil this mistake down to one piece of advice: Always be ready and willing to buy back short strategies early. When a trade is going your way, it can be easy to rest on your laurels and assume it will continue to do so. But remember, this will not always be the case. A trade that's working in your favor can just as easily turn south.

There are a million excuses traders give themselves for waiting too long to buy back options they've sold: I'm betting the contract will expire worthless, I don't want to pay the commission to get out of the position, I'm hoping to eke just a little more profit out of the trade…the list goes on and on.

HOW YOU CAN TRADE SMARTER

If your short option gets way out-of-the-money and you can buy it back to take the risk off the table profitably, then do it. Don't be cheap.

Here's my personal rule: if I can keep 80% or more of my initial gain from the sale of an option, I'll buy it back immediately and I suggest you do the same. Otherwise, I promise that one of these days, a short option will come back and bite you when you've waited too long to close your position.

For example, if you sold a short strategy for $1.00 and you can buy it back for 20 cents a week before expiration, you should jump on the opportunity. Very rarely will it be worth an extra week of risk just to hang onto a measly 20 cents.

This is also the case with higher-dollar trades, but the rule can be harder to stick to. If you sold a strategy for $5.00 and it would cost $1.00 to close, it can be even more tempting to stay in your position. But think about the risk / reward. Option trades can go south in a hurry. So by spending the 20% to close out trades and manage your risk, you can save yourself many painful slaps to the forehead.

MISTAKE 5: LEGGING INTO SPREAD TRADES

"Legging in" is when you enter the different legs of a multi-leg trade one at a time. If you're trading a long call spread, for example, you might be tempted to buy the long call first and then try to time the sale of the short call with an uptick in the stock price to squeeze another nickel or two out of the second leg.

However, oftentimes the market will downtick instead, and you won't be able to pull off your spread at all. Now you're stuck with a long call with no way to hedge your risk.

HOW YOU CAN TRADE SMARTER

Unfortunately, I must admit I've legged into spreads before. But please do as I say, not as I used to do.

I learned my lesson the hard way. But learning your lesson the easy way (by reading this playbook) is a whole heck of a lot cheaper. Always enter a spread as a single trade. It's just foolish to take on extra market risk needlessly.

When you use TradeKing's spread trading screen, you can be sure all legs of your trade are sent to market simultaneously, and we won't execute your spread unless we can achieve the net debit or credit you're looking for. It's simply a smarter way to execute your strategy and avoid any extra risk.

(Just keep in mind that multi-leg strategies are subject to additional risks and multiple commissions and may be subject to particular tax consequences. Please consult with your tax advisor prior to engaging in these strategies.)

SO WHAT'S AN INDEX OPTION, ANYHOW?

Like stock options, index option prices rise or fall based on several factors, like the value of the underlying security, strike price, volatility, time until expiration, interest rates and dividends. But there are five important ways index options differ from stock options, and it's important to understand these differences before you can start trading index options.

Let's have a look at these differences, shall we?

DIFFERENCE 1: MULTIPLE UNDERLYING STOCKS VS. A SINGLE UNDERLYING STOCK

Whereas stock options are based on a single company's stock, index options are based on a basket of stocks representing either a broad or a narrow band of the overall market.

Narrow-based indexes are based on specific sectors like semiconductors or the financial industry, and tend to be composed of relatively few stocks. Broad-based indexes have many different industries represented by their component companies. But that doesn't necessarily mean there are a ton of stocks that make up a particular broad index.

For instance, the Dow Jones Industrial Average is a broad-based index that's only composed of 30 stocks, but it still represents a broad range of sectors. As you would expect, however, other broad-based indexes are indeed made up of many different stocks. The S&P 500 is a good example of that.

DIFFERENCE 2: SETTLEMENT METHOD

When stock options are exercised, the underlying stock is required to change hands. But index options are cash-settled instead.

If you exercise a call option based on the S&P 500, you don't have to buy all 500 stocks in the index. That would be ridiculous. The index value is just a gauge to determine how much the option is worth at any given time.

DIFFERENCE 3: SETTLEMENT STYLE

As of this writing, all stock options have American-style exercise, meaning they can be exercised at any point before expiration. Most index options, on the other hand, have European-style exercise. So they can't be exercised until expiration.

But that doesn't mean that if you buy an index option, you're stuck with it until expiration. As with any other option, you can buy or sell to close your position at any time throughout the life of the contract.

DIFFERENCE 4: SETTLEMENT DATE

The last day to trade stock options is the third Friday of the month, and settlement is determined on Saturday. The last day to trade index options is usually the Thursday before the third Friday of the month, followed by determination of the settlement value on Friday. The settlement value is then compared to the strike price of the option to see how much, if any, cash will change hands between the option buyer and seller.

DIFFERENCE 5: TRADING HOURS

Stock options and narrow-based index options stop trading at 4:00 ET, whereas broad-based indexes stop trading at 4:15 ET. If a piece of news came out immediately after the stock market close, it might have a significant impact on the value of stock options and narrow-based index options. However, since there are so many different sectors in broad-based indexes, this is not so much of a concern.

NOW FOR THE DISCLAIMER:

All of these are very general characteristics of indexes. In practice, there are lots of small exceptions to these general rules. For example, the OEX (that's the ticker symbol for the S&P 100) is one big exception. Although the OEX is an index, options traded on it have American-style exercise.

In the table to the right I've highlighted a few of the general differences between index options and stock options. But make sure you do your homework before trading any index option so you know the type of settlement and the settlement date.

👤 OPTIONS GUY'S TIP:

☞ As you read through the plays, you probably noticed that I mentioned indexes are popular for neutral-based trades like condors. That's because historically, indexes have not been as volatile as many individual stocks. Fluctuations in an index's component stock prices tend to cancel one another out, lessening the volatility of the index as a whole.

DIFFERENT STROKES FOR DIFFERENT UNDERLYING SECURITIES

	INDEX BROAD OPTIONS	INDEX NARROW OPTIONS	STOCK OPTIONS	ETF OPTIONS
SETTLEMENT METHOD	Cash	Cash	Shares	ETF shares
LAST DAY OF TRADING	Thursday before 3rd Friday	Thursday or Friday	Friday	Friday
EXERCISE STYLE	Usually European, occasionally American	Sometimes European, sometimes American	American	American
WHEN SETTLED	Usually AM, occasionally PM	Sometimes AM, sometimes PM	PM	PM
MARKET CLOSE	4:15	4:00	4:00	4:15
EXPIRATION DATE	3rd Friday (except weekly & quarterly options)	3rd Friday	3rd Friday	3rd Friday (except quarterly options)

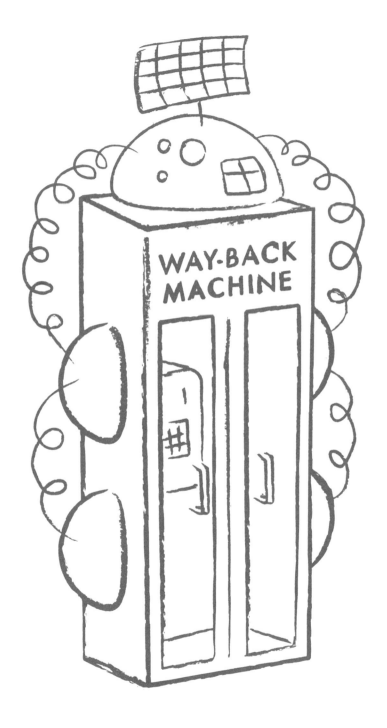

A BRIEF HISTORY OF OPTIONS

There are plenty of good option traders who don't know anything about the following historical facts. But I've included this section of the book for those inquisitive souls with the drive to learn everything possible about whatever subject they choose to study.

If you fall into that category, I salute you. Join me in the trusty Way-back Machine and let's examine the evolution of the modern-day options market.

TIPTOE THROUGH THE TULIP MARKET OF THE 1600s

Nowadays, options are often used successfully as an instrument for speculation and for hedging risk. But the options market didn't always function quite as smoothly as it does today. Let's begin our foray into options history with a look at the debacle commonly referred to as the "Tulip Bulb Mania" of 17th-century Holland.

In the early 1600s, tulips were extremely popular as a status symbol among the Dutch aristocracy. And as their popularity began to spill across Holland's borders to a worldwide market, prices went up dramatically.

To hedge risk in case of a bad harvest, tulip wholesalers began to buy call options, and tulip growers began to protect profits with put options. At first, the trading of options in Holland seemed like perfectly reasonable economic activity. But as the price of tulip bulbs continued to rise, the value of existing option contracts increased dramatically. So a secondary market for those option contracts emerged among the general public. In fact, it was not unheard of for families to use their entire fortunes to speculate on the tulip bulb market.

Unfortunately, when the Dutch economy slipped into recession in 1638, the bubble burst and the price of tulips plummeted. Many of the speculators who had sold put options were either unable or unwilling to fulfill their obligations. To make matters worse, the options market in 17th-century Holland was entirely unregulated. So despite the Dutch government's efforts to force speculators to make good on their option contracts, you can't get blood from a stone. (Or a dried-up, withered tulip bulb, for that matter.)

So thousands of ordinary Hollanders lost more than their frilly-collared shirts. They also lost their petticoat breeches, buckled hats, canal-side mansions, windmills and untold herds of farm animals in the process. And options managed to acquire a bad reputation that would last for almost three centuries.

THE BIRTH OF THE U.S. OPTIONS MARKET

In 1791, the New York Stock Exchange opened. And it wasn't long before a market for stock options began to emerge among savvy investors.

However, in those days, a centralized marketplace for options didn't exist. Options were traded "over the counter," facilitated by broker-dealers who tried to match option sellers with option buyers. Each underlying stock strike price, expiration date and cost had to be individually negotiated.

By the late 1800s, broker-dealers began to place advertisements in financial journals on the part of potential option buyers and sellers, in hopes of attracting another interested party. So advertisements were the seed that eventually germinated into the option quote page in financial journals. But back then it was quite a cumbersome process to arrange an option contract: Place an ad in the newspaper and wait for the phone to ring.

Eventually, the formation of the Put and Call Brokers and Dealers Association, Inc., helped to establish networks that could match option buyers and sellers more efficiently. But further problems arose due to the lack of standardized pricing in the options market. The terms of each option contract still had to be determined between the buyer and seller.

For example, in the year 1895, you might have seen an advertisement for Bob's Put Call Broker-Dealer in a financial journal. You could then call Bob on your old-timey telephone and say, "I'm bullish on Acme Buggy Whips, Inc., and I want to buy a call option."

Bob would check the current price for Acme Buggy Whips stock – say 21 3/8 – and that would usually become your strike price. (Back in those days, most options would initially be traded at-the-money.) Then, you would need to mutually agree on the expiration date, perhaps three weeks from the day you placed the phone call. You could then offer Bob a dollar for the option, and Bob would say, "Sorry pal, but I want two bucks."

After a bit of haggling, you might arrive at 1 5/8 as the cost of the option. Bob would then either try to match you up with a seller for the option contract, or if he thought it was favorable enough he might take the other side of the trade himself. At that point, you'd have to sign the contract in order to make it valid.

A big problem arose, however, because there was no liquidity in the options market. Once you owned the option, you'd either have to wait to see what happened at expiration, ask Bob to buy the option back from you, or place a new ad in a financial journal in order to resell it.

Furthermore, as in 17th-century Holland, there still existed quite a bit of risk that sellers of option contracts wouldn't fulfill their obligations. If you did manage to establish a profitable option position and the counterparty didn't have the means to fulfill the terms of a contract you exercised, you were out of luck. There was still no easy way to force the counterparty to pay up.

THE EMERGENCE OF THE LISTED OPTIONS MARKET

After the stock market crash of 1929, Congress decided to intervene in the financial marketplace. They created the Securities and Exchange Commission (SEC), which became the regulating authority under the Securities and Exchange Act of 1934.

In 1935, shortly after the SEC began regulating the over-the-counter options market, it granted the Chicago Board of Trade (CBOT) a license to register as a national securities exchange. The license was written with no expiration, which turned out to be a very good thing because it took the CBOT more than three decades to act on it.

In 1968, low volume in the commodity futures market forced CBOT to look for other ways of expanding its business. It was decided to create an open-outcry exchange for stock options, modeled after the method for trading futures. So the Chicago Board Option Exchange (CBOE) was created as a spin-off entity from the CBOT.

As opposed to the over-the-counter options market, which had no set terms, this new exchange set up rules to standardize contract size, strike price and expiration dates. They also established centralized clearing.

Further contributing to the viability of a listed option exchange, in 1973 Fischer Black and Myron Scholes published an article titled "The Pricing of Options and Corporate Liabilities" in the **University of Chicago's Journal of Political Economy**. The Black-Scholes formula was based on an equation from thermodynamic physics and could be used to derive a theoretical price for financial instruments with a known expiration date.

It was immediately adopted in the marketplace as the standard for evaluating the price relationships of options, and its publication was of tremendous importance to the evolution of the modern-day options market. In fact, Black and Scholes were later awarded a Nobel Prize in Economics for their contribution to options pricing (and hopefully drank a lot of aquavit to celebrate during the trip to Sweden to pick up their prize).

SOME BUSINESSES START IN A BASEMENT. THE CBOE STARTED IN A SMOKER'S LOUNGE.

1973 also saw the birth of the Options Clearing Corporation (OCC), which was created to ensure that the obligations associated with options contracts are fulfilled in a timely and reliable manner. And so it was that on April 26 of that year, the opening bell sounded on the Chicago Board Option Exchange (CBOE).

Although today it is a large and prestigious organization, the CBOE had rather humble origins. Believe it or not, the original exchange was located in the former smoker's lounge of the Chicago Board of Trade Building. (Traders used to smoke a lot in the old days, so at least it was a fairly big smoker's lounge.)

Many questioned the wisdom of opening a new securities exchange in the midst of one of the worst bear markets on record. Still others doubted the ability of "grain traders in Chicago" to market a financial instrument that was generally considered far too complicated for the general public to understand. Too bad *The Options Playbook* didn't exist back then, or the latter wouldn't have been much of a concern.

On opening day, the CBOE only allowed trading of call options on a scant 16 underlying stocks. However, a somewhat respectable 911 contracts changed hands, and by the end of the month the CBOE's average daily volume exceeded that of the over-the-counter option market.

By June 1974, the CBOE average daily volume reached over 20,000 contracts. And the exponential growth of the options market over the first year proved to be a portent of things to come. In 1975, the Philadelphia Stock Exchange and American Stock Exchange opened their own option trading floors, increasing competition and bringing options to a wider marketplace.

In 1977, the CBOE increased the number of stocks on which options were traded to 43 and began to allow put trading on a few stocks in addition to calls.

THE SEC STEPS IN

Due to the explosive growth of the options market, in 1977 the SEC decided to conduct a complete review of the structure and regulatory practices of all option exchanges. They put a moratorium on listing options for additional stocks and discussed whether or not it was desirable or viable to create a centralized options market.

By 1980, the SEC had put in place new regulations regarding market surveillance at exchanges, consumer protection and compliance systems at brokerage houses. Finally they lifted the moratorium, and the CBOE responded by adding options on 25 more stocks.

GROWING IN LEAPS AND BOUNDS

The next major event was in 1983, when index options began to trade. This development proved critical in helping to fuel the popularity of the options industry. The first index options were traded on the CBOE 100 index, which was later renamed the S&P 100 (OEX). Four months later, options began trading on the S&P 500 index (SPX). Today, there are upwards of 50 different index options, and since 1983 more than 1 billion contracts have been traded.

1990 saw another crucial event, with the introduction of Long-term Equity AnticiPation Securities (LEAPS). These options have a shelf life of up to three years, enabling investors to take advantage of longer-term trends in the market. Today, LEAPS are available on more than 2,500 different securities.

In the mid-'90s, web-based online trading started to become popular, making options instantly accessible to members of the general public. Long, long gone were the days of haggling over the terms of individual option contracts. This was a brand-new era of instant options gratification, with quotes available on demand, covering options on a dizzying array of securities with a wide range of strike prices and expiration dates.

WHERE WE STAND TODAY

The emergence of computerized trading systems and the internet has created a far more viable and liquid options market than ever before. Because of this, we've seen several new players enter the marketplace. As of this writing, the listed options exchanges in the United States include the Boston Stock Exchange, Chicago Board Options Exchange, International Securities Exchange, NASDAQ OMX PHLX, NASDAQ Stock Market, NYSE Amex and NYSE Arca.

Thus, today it's remarkably easy for any investor to place an option trade (especially if you do so with TradeKing). There are an average of more than 11 million option contracts traded every day on more than 3,000 securities, and the market just continues to grow. And thanks to the vast array of internet resources and books like the one you are currently reading, the general public has a better understanding of options than ever before.

In December 2005, the most important event in the history of options occurred, namely, the introduction of TradeKing to the investing public. In fact, in my humble opinion this was arguably the single most important event in the history of the universe, with the possible exception of the Big Bang and the invention of the beer cozy. But I'm not really sure about those last two.

APPENDICES

APPENDIX A: MARGIN REQUIREMENTS

When running some of the option plays in this book, you need to keep cash in your account in case the trade goes against you. So I've indicated the initial margin for plays that have any requirement beyond the cost to establish the trade.

After the position is established, ongoing maintenance margin requirements may apply. That means depending on how your options perform, an increase (or decrease) in the required margin is possible.

Keep in mind these requirements are subject to change. Furthermore, they're listed on a per-contract basis. So don't forget to multiply by the total number of units when you're doing the math.

If you have any questions about your margin requirements, feel free to talk with TradeKing Customer Service at (877) 495-KING.

SHORT CALL

Margin requirement is the greater of the following:

» 25% of the underlying security value minus the out-of-the-money amount (if any), plus the premium received.

OR 10% of the underlying security value plus the premium received.

NOTE: The premium received from establishing the short call may be applied to the initial margin requirement.

SHORT PUT

Margin requirement is the greater of the following:

» 25% of underlying security value minus the out-of-the-money amount (if any), plus the premium received.

OR 10% of the strike price of the put option plus the premium received.

NOTE: The premium received from establishing the short put may be applied to the initial margin requirement.

CASH-SECURED PUT

You must have enough cash to cover the cost of purchasing the stock at the strike price.

NOTE: The premium received from establishing the short put may be applied to the initial margin requirement.

SHORT CALL SPREAD

Margin requirement is the difference between the strike prices.

NOTE: The net credit received when establishing the short call spread may be applied to the initial margin requirement.

SHORT PUT SPREAD

Margin requirement is the difference between the strike prices.

NOTE: The net credit received when establishing the short put spread may be applied to the initial margin requirement.

SHORT STRADDLE

Margin requirement is the short call or short put requirement (whichever is greater), plus the premium received from the other side.

NOTE: The net credit received from establishing the short straddle may be applied to the initial margin requirement.

SHORT STRANGLE

Margin requirement is the short call or short put requirement (whichever is greater), plus the credit received from the other side.

NOTE: The net credit received from establishing the short strangle may be applied to the initial margin requirement.

LONG COMBINATION

Margin requirement is the short put requirement.

NOTE: If established for a net credit, the proceeds may be applied to the initial margin requirement.

SHORT COMBINATION

Margin requirement is the short call requirement.

NOTE: If established for a net credit, the proceeds may be applied to the initial margin requirement.

FRONT SPREAD WITH CALLS

Margin requirement is equal to the requirement for the uncovered short call portion of the front spread.

NOTE: If established for a net credit, the proceeds may be applied to the initial margin requirement.

FRONT SPREAD WITH PUTS

Margin requirement is equal to the requirement for the uncovered short put portion of the front spread.

NOTE: If established for a net credit, the proceeds may be applied to the initial margin requirement.

BACK SPREAD WITH CALLS

Margin requirement is equal to the difference between the strike prices of the short call spread embedded into this strategy.

NOTE: If established for a net credit, the proceeds may be applied to the initial margin requirement.

BACK SPREAD WITH PUTS

Margin requirement is equal to the difference between the strike prices of the short put spread embedded into this strategy.

NOTE: If established for a net credit, the proceeds may be applied to the initial margin requirement.

DIAGONAL SPREAD WITH CALLS

Margin requirement is the difference between the strike prices (if the position is closed at expiration of the front-month option).

NOTE: If established for a net credit, the proceeds may be applied to the initial margin requirement.

DIAGONAL SPREAD WITH PUTS

Margin requirement is the difference between the strike prices (if the position is closed at expiration of the front-month option).

NOTE: If established for a net credit, the proceeds may be applied to the initial margin requirement.

IRON BUTTERFLY

Margin requirement is the greater of the following:

» The short call spread requirement.

OR The short put spread requirement.

NOTE: The net credit received when establishing the iron butterfly may be applied to the initial margin requirement.

SKIP STRIKE BUTTERFLY WITH CALLS

Margin requirement is equal to the difference between the strike prices of the short call spread embedded into this strategy.

NOTE: If established for a net credit, the proceeds may be applied to the initial margin requirement.

SKIP STRIKE BUTTERFLY WITH PUTS

Margin requirement is equal to the difference between the strike prices of the short put spread embedded into this strategy.

NOTE: If established for a net credit, the proceeds may be applied to the initial margin requirement.

INVERSE SKIP STRIKE BUTTERFLY WITH CALLS

Margin requirement is equal to the difference between the strike prices of the short call spread embedded into this strategy.

NOTE: If established for a net credit, the proceeds may be applied to the initial margin requirement.

INVERSE SKIP STRIKE BUTTERFLY WITH PUTS

Margin requirement is equal to the difference between the strike prices of the short put spread embedded into this strategy.

NOTE: If established for a net credit, the proceeds may be applied to the initial margin requirement.

IRON CONDOR

Margin requirement is the greater of the following:

» The short call spread requirement.

OR The short put spread requirement.

NOTE: The net credit received when establishing the iron condor may be applied to the initial margin requirement.

DOUBLE DIAGONAL

Margin requirement is the greater of the following (if the position is closed at expiration of the front-month option):

» The call diagonal spread requirement.

OR The put diagonal spread requirement.

NOTE: If established for a net credit, the proceeds may be applied to the initial margin requirement.

APPENDIX B: GLOSSARY

(AKA DEFINITELY BORING DEFINITIONS)

Sometimes when defining terms throughout the playbook, I simplified things a little so they'd be easier to understand. But here I present the standard textbook definitions for a whole slew of options terminology without any jokes, interjections or unnecessary asides.

If your friends like to refer to you as "Poindexter" and that is not your real name, I'm sure you'll enjoy these definitions much more than the ones in the front of the book.

ASSIGNMENT

The receipt of an exercise notice by an equity option seller (writer) that obligates him/her to sell (in the case of a short call) or buy (in the case of a short put) 100 shares of underlying stock at the strike price per share.

AT-THE-MONEY

An equity call or put option is at-the-money when its strike price is the same as the current underlying stock price.

BACK MONTH

For an option spread involving two expiration months, the month that is farther away in time.

BREAK-EVEN POINT

An underlying stock price at which an option strategy will realize neither a profit nor a loss, generally at option expiration.

CALL OPTION

An equity option that gives its buyer the right to buy 100 shares of the underlying stock at the strike price per share at any time before it expires. The call seller (or writer), on the other hand, has the obligation to sell 100 shares at the strike price if called upon to do so.

CASH SETTLEMENT

A settlement style that is generally characteristic of index options. Instead of stock changing hands after a call or put is exercised (physical settlement), cash changes hands. When an in-the-money contract is exercised, a cash equivalent of the option's intrinsic value is paid to the option holder by the option seller (writer) who is assigned.

CLOSING TRANSACTION

A transaction that eliminates (or reduces) an open option position. A closing sell transaction eliminates or reduces a long position. A closing buy transaction eliminates or reduces a short position.

COMMISSION

The fee charged by a brokerage firm for its services in the execution of a stock or option order on a securities exchange.

COST-TO-CARRY

The total costs involved with establishing and maintaining an option and/or stock position, such as interest paid on a margined long stock position or dividends owed for a short stock position.

CREDIT (TRANSACTION)

Any cash received in an account from the sale of an option or stock position. With a complex strategy involving multiple parts (legs), a net credit transaction is one in which the total cash amount received is greater than the total cash amount paid.

DEBIT (TRANSACTION)

Any cash paid out of an account for the purchase of an option or stock position. With a complex strategy involving multiple parts (legs), a net debit transaction is one in which the total cash amount paid is greater than the total cash amount received.

DELTA

The amount a theoretical option's price will change for a corresponding one-unit (point) change in the price of the underlying security.

EARLY EXERCISE / ASSIGNMENT

The exercise or assignment of an option contract before its expiration. This is a feature of American-style options that may be exercised or assigned at any time before they expire.

EQUITY OPTION

A contract that gives its buyer (owner) the right, but not the obligation, to either buy or sell 100 shares of a specific underlying stock or exchange-traded fund (ETF) at a specific price (strike or exercise price) per share, at any time before the contract expires.

EVEN MONEY (TRANSACTION)

With a complex strategy involving multiple parts (legs), an even money transaction results when the total cash amount received is the same as the total cash amount paid.

EXCHANGE TRADED FUND (ETF)

A security that represents shares of ownership in a fund or investment trust that holds a basket (collection) of specific component stocks. ETF shares are listed and traded on securities exchanges just like stock, and so may be bought and sold throughout the trading day.

EX-DIVIDEND DATE

When a corporation declares a dividend, it will simultaneously declare a "record date" on which an investor must be recorded into the company's books as a shareholder to receive that dividend. Also included in the declaration is the "payable date," which comes after the record date, and is the actual date dividend payments are made. Once these dates are established, the exchanges will then set the "ex-dividend" date ("ex-date") for two business days prior to the record date. If you buy stock before the ex-dividend date, you will be eligible to receive the upcoming dividend payment. If you buy stock on the ex-date or afterwards, you will not receive the dividend.

EXERCISE

To employ the rights an equity option contract conveys to its buyer to either buy (in the case of a call) or sell (in the case of a put) 100 shares of the underlying security at the strike price per share at any time before the contract expires.

EXERCISE PRICE

A term of any equity option contract, it is the price per share at which shares of stock will change hands after an option is exercised or assigned. Also referred to as the "strike price," or simply the "strike."

EXPIRATION DATE

The day on which an option contract literally expires and ceases to exist. For equity options, this is the Saturday following the third Friday of the expiration month. The last day on which expiring equity options trade and may be exercised is the business day prior to the expiration date, or generally the third Friday of the month.

EXPIRATION MONTH

The calendar month during which a specific expiration date occurs.

EXTRINSIC VALUE

The portion of an option's premium (price) that exceeds its intrinsic value, if it is in-the-money. If the option is out-of-the-money, the extrinsic value is equal to the entire premium. Also known as "time value."

FRONT MONTH

For an option spread involving two expiration months, the month that is nearer in time.

GAMMA

The amount a theoretical option's delta will change for a corresponding one-unit (point) change in the price of the underlying security.

HISTORICAL VOLATILITY

A measurement of the actual observed volatility of a specific stock over a given period of time in the past, such as a month, quarter or year.

IMPLIED VOLATILITY

An estimate of an underlying stock's future volatility as predicted or implied by an option's current market price. Implied volatility for any option can only be determined via an option pricing model.

INDEX OPTION

An option contract whose underlying security is an index (like the NASDAQ), not shares of any particular stock.

IN-THE-MONEY

An equity call contract is in-the-money when its strike price is less than the current underlying stock price. An equity put contract is in-the-money when its strike price is greater than the current underlying stock price.

INTRINSIC VALUE

The in-the-money portion (if any) of a call or put contract's current market price.

LEAPS

Long-term Equity AnticiPation Securities, or LEAPS, are long-term option contracts. Equity LEAPS calls and puts can have expirations up to three years into the future and expire in January of their expiration years.

LEG

1: One part of a complex position composed of two or more different options and/or a position in the underlying stock

2: Instead of entering one order to establish all parts of a complex position simultaneously, one part is executed with the hope of establishing the other part(s) later at a better price.

LOGNORMAL DISTRIBUTION

With respect to stock prices over a period of time, a lognormal distribution of daily price changes represents not the actual dollar amount of each change, but instead the logarithms of each change. Mathematically, this type of distribution implies that a stock's price can only range between 0 and infinity, which in the real world is the case. So in a sense a lognormal distribution could be considered to have a bullish bias. A stock can only drop 100% in value but can increase by more than 100%. In general, assumptions made by option pricing models about a stock's future volatility are based on a lognormal distribution of future price changes.

LONG OPTION

A position resulting from the opening purchase of a call or put contract and held (owned) in a brokerage account.

LONG STOCK

Shares of stock that are purchased and held in a brokerage account and which represent an equity interest in the company that issued the shares.

MARGIN REQUIREMENT

The amount of cash and/or securities an option writer is required to deposit and maintain in a brokerage account to cover an uncovered (naked) short option position. This cash can be seen as collateral pledged to the brokerage firm for the writer's obligation to buy (in the case of a put) or sell (in the case of a call) shares of underlying stock in case of assignment.

MEAN

For a data set, the mean is the sum of the observations divided by the number of observations. The mean is often quoted along with the standard deviation: the mean describes the central location of the data, and the standard deviation describes the range of possible occurrences.

NORMAL DISTRIBUTION

One of the most familiar mathematical distributions, it is a set of random observed numbers (or closing stock prices) whose distribution is symmetrical around the mean or average number. A graph of the distribution is the familiar "bell curve," with the most frequently occurring numbers clustered around the mean, or the middle of the bell. Since this a symmetrical distribution, when the numbers represent daily stock price changes, for every possible change to the upside there must be an equal price change to the downside. The result is that a normal distribution would theoretically allow negative stock prices. Stock prices are unlimited to the upside, but in the real world a stock can only decline to zero. See "lognormal distribution."

OPENING TRANSACTION

A transaction that creates (or increases) an open option position. An opening buy transaction creates or increases a long position; an opening sell transaction creates or increases a short position (also known as writing).

OPTION PRICING MODEL

A mathematical formula used to calculate an option's theoretical value using as input its strike price, the underlying stock's price, volatility and dividend amount, as well as time until expiration and risk-free interest rate. Generated by an option pricing model are the Greeks: delta, gamma, theta, vega and rho. Well-known and widely used pricing models include the Black-Scholes, Cox-Ross-Rubinstein and Roll-Geske-Whaley.

OUT-OF-THE-MONEY

An equity call option is out-of-the-money when its strike price is greater than the current underlying stock price. An equity put option is out-of-the-money when its strike price is less than the current underlying stock price.

PHYSICAL SETTLEMENT

The settlement style of all equity options in which shares of underlying stock change hands when an option is exercised.

PREMIUM

The price paid or received for an option in the marketplace. Equity option premiums are quoted on a price-per-share basis, so the total premium amount paid by the buyer to the seller in any option transaction is equal to the quoted amount times 100 (underlying shares). Option premium consists of intrinsic value (if any) plus time value.

PROFIT + LOSS GRAPH

A representation in graph format of the possible profit and loss outcomes of an equity option strategy over a range of underlying stock prices at a given point in the future, most commonly at option expiration.

PUT OPTION

An equity option that gives its buyer the right to sell 100 shares of the underlying stock at the strike price per share at any time before it expires. The put seller (or writer), on the other hand, has the obligation to buy 100 shares at the strike price if called upon to do so.

RHO

The amount a theoretical option's price will change for a corresponding one-unit (percentage-point) change in the interest rate used to price the option contract.

ROLL

To simultaneously close one option position and open another with the same underlying stock but a different strike price and/or expiration month. Rolling a long position involves selling those options and buying others. Rolling a short position involves buying the existing position and selling (writing) other options to create a new short position.

SHORT OPTION

A position resulting from making the opening sale (or writing) of a call or put contract, which is then maintained in a brokerage account.

SHORT STOCK

A short position that is opened by selling shares in the marketplace that are not currently owned (short sale), but instead borrowed from a broker/dealer. At a later date, shares must be purchased and returned to the lending broker/dealer to close the short position. If the shares can be purchased at a price lower than their initial sale, a profit will result. If the shares are purchased at a higher price, a loss will be incurred. Unlimited losses are possible when taking a short stock position.

SPREAD

A complex option position established by the purchase of one option and the sale of another option with the same underlying security. The two options may be of the same or different types (calls/puts), and may have the same or different strike prices and/or expiration months. A spread order is executed as a package, with both parts (legs) traded simultaneously, at a net debit, net credit, or for even money.

STRIKE PRICE

A term of any equity option contract, it is the price per share at which shares of stock will change hands after an option is exercised or assigned. Also referred to as the "exercise price," or simply the "strike."

THETA

The amount a theoretical option's price will change for a corresponding one-unit (day) change in the days to expiration of the option contract.

TIME DECAY (EROSION)

A regular phenomenon in which the time value portion of an option's price decays (decreases) with the passage of time. The rate of this decay increases as expiration gets closer, with the theoretical rate quantified by "theta," one of the Greeks.

TIME VALUE

For a call or put, it is the portion of the option's premium (price) that exceeds its intrinsic value (in-the-money amount), if it has any. By definition, the premium of at- and out-of-the-money options consists only of time value. It is time value that is affected by time decay as well as changing volatility, interest rates and dividends.

UNDERLYING STOCK

The stock on which a specific equity option's value is based, which changes hands when the option is exercised or assigned.

VEGA

The amount a theoretical option's price will change for a corresponding one-unit (point) change in the implied volatility of the option contract.

VOLATILITY

The fluctuation, up or down, in the price of a stock. It is measured mathematically as the annualized standard deviation of that stock's daily price changes.

WRITE

To sell a call or put option contract that has not already been purchased (owned). This is known as an opening sale transaction and results in a short position in that option. The seller (writer) of an equity option is subject to assignment at any time before expiration and takes on an obligation to sell (in the case of a short call) or buy (in the case of a short put) underlying stock if assignment does occur.

**CONGRATULATIONS ON MAKING
IT ALL THE WAY TO THE END OF
THE OPTIONS PLAYBOOK.™**

By now, your head must be so full of option-related knowledge you probably need a bigger hat. Hopefully, you're also well on your way to making smarter trades.

If your mental hard drive isn't quite full, check out my blog in the TradeKing Trader Network. I'm constantly updating it with information that you'll find useful when placing your trades. And don't forget to refer back to this playbook while considering which strategy to run.

Now, in parting, I'd like to leave you with one simple wish:

*May all the options you buy expire
in-the-money, and all the ones you sell
expire out-of-the-money.*

Happy Trading,

Brian Overby

ACKNOWLEDGEMENTS

Special thanks to the crew at Stick and Move in Philadelphia for all their hard work from day one. They helped with the conception of *The Options Playbook*, did the layout and production and pretty much supported me every step of the way.

I would also like to show appreciation to my friend and mentor Jim Bittman, just for being Jim Bittman. He did not have a hands-on involvement in this book, but contributed immensely with his willingness to share his vast options knowledge throughout our many years of friendship.

Thanks also go – in alphabetical order – to Jude Stewart (TradeKing Director of Online Content) and Nicole Wachs (TradeKing Director of Education) for their editorial assistance. You were a huge help.

A thousand truckloads of thanks to everybody else on the TradeKing team who helped make this book possible. You know who you are, and you rock.